The Ultimate Audition Book
for Teens Volume V

ONE HUNDRED
AND ELEVEN
SHAKESPEARE
MONOLOGUES

Edited by Lisa Bansavage and
L. E. McCullough

Introduction by Jill K. Swanson

YOUNG ACTORS SERIES

A Smith and Kraus Book

A Smith and Kraus Book
Published by Smith and Kraus, Inc.
177 Lyme Road, Hanover, NH 03755
www.smithkraus.com

First Edition: May 2003
Manufactured in the United States of America
10 9 8 7 6 5 4 3 2 1

Cover and text design by Julia Gignoux, Freedom Hill Design

Library of Congress Cataloging-in-Publication Data
Shakespeare, William, 1564–1616.
[Plays. Selections]
One hundred and eleven Shakespeare monologues for teens / [compiled]
by Lisa Bansavage and L.E. McCullough ; with a special introduction
on Shakespearean speech by Jill K. Swanson. —1st ed.
p. cm. (Young actors series)
Contents: Women's monologues — Men's monologues.
ISBN 1-57525-356-9
1. Shakespeare, William, 1564–1616—Quotations. 2. Young adult drama, English.
3. Acting—Auditions. 4. Monologues. [1. Shakespeare, William, 1564–1616—
Quotations. 2. Acting—Auditions. 3. Monologues. 4. English drama—17th century.]
I. Title: 111 Shakespeare monologues for teens. II. Bansavage, Lisa. III. McCullough, L. E. IV. Swanson, Jill K. V. Title. VI. Young actors series.

PR2771.B36 2003
822.3'3—dc21
2003042785

To actors everywhere who have followed their spirit,
stiffened the sinews, summoned up the blood, and
plunged once more into the breach.

THE ULTIMATE AUDITION BOOK FOR TEENS SERIES

The Ultimate Audition Book for Teens Volume 1: 111 One-Minute
Monologues by Janet Milstein

The Ultimate Audition Book for Teens Volume 2: 111 One-Minute
Monologues by L. E. McCullough

The Ultimate Audition Book for Teens Volume 4: 111 One-Minute
Monologues by Debbie Lamedman

THE ULTIMATE SCENE STUDY SERIES FOR TEENS

The Ultimate Scene Study Series for Teens Volume 1:
60 Shakespeare Scenes

The Ultimate Scene Study Series for Teens Volume 2:
60 Original Scenes

ACKNOWLEDGMENTS

LISA BANSAVAGE would like to acknowledge The Stratford, Ontario Shakespeare Festival for inspiring me as a teenager; Carnegie Mellon University and the conservatory training I received there; Director Patrick Tucker for awakening me to the joys of working from the First Folio; my parents, Judith and Joseph Bansavage, for exposing me as a child to great theater; all the wonderful actors I've had the pleasure of performing with who share a love of Shakespeare.

JILL K. SWANSON would like to acknowledge Anne Towns; Daniel Wilson, Austin Shakespeare Festival; Jean McDaniel, Florida State University; Ann Ciccolella, Zachary Scott Theatre; Elizabeth Hansing-Moon, St. Stephen's Episcopal School; Bill and Jeanne Swanson.

L. E. MCCULLOUGH would like to acknowledge *MacBird!* by Barbara Garson, the modern fable in Shakespearean clothing that sparked my interest in theater as a vehicle for social commentary and proved the Bard created timeless drama for every age; my parents, Isabel and Ervin McCullough, who gave me my first glimpse of theater at the old Starlight Musicals (R.I.P.); my wife, Lisa Bansavage — the light that breaks through yonder window of my soul.

CONTENTS

FEMALE MONOLOGUES

COMEDIES

HISTORIES

TRAGEDIES

MALE MONOLOGUES

COMEDIES

HISTORIES

TRAGEDIES

FEMALE OR MALE MONOLOGUES

INTRODUCTION
SHAKESPEAREAN SPEECH AND ACTING

> You know, Hamlet's Speech To The Players is it, because our job is to hold the mirror up to nature. If it's funny, that's fine, if it entertains you, that's fine. But it must, under all circumstances, hold the mirror up to nature. We must constantly be examining who we are, how we got here, and how we're getting through all of this.
>
> — *Tom Hanks, actor/director*

So you're doing a Shakespearean speech! That scares the pants off of everyone, kids and professional actors alike. Why? Because he's been dead for almost four hundred years? Because his characters "talk funny"? Because someone told you that his works are "poetry" and you can't imagine how to *act* poetry? For most of us, it's all of the above. But Shakespeare tells stories of love, jealousy, anger, war, greed, guilt, fear, and what it means to be human. Turns out, he's not that different from us after all.

And the words! The words and images that his characters use to tell you these heart-stopping stories may seem foreign, but they were almost as foreign to Elizabethan audiences as they are to us today. He was a genius, coming up with ways to engage and entertain us through words in a way that no one had ever done before. The English language was not broad enough to do what he wanted, so he made up words (some of which are still in common use) and wove them into the most unique patterns to not only tell us the story but also to create for his audience a world that didn't exist.

How do we create fake realities for plays, films, and TV today? We build sets to look like different environments, and in film and TV computers generate some of the backgrounds or even crowd scenes. We set the lights to show if it's day or night, outside or indoors. We dress the actors up in costumes that are often so realistic one can't tell them from the real thing. We fill the sets with realistic props to make the environment seem lived-in. We play music to set the mood, or to clue the audience in to an important moment, and we put the audience in a dark, quiet room where they can see and hear nothing but us.

There were no sets in Shakespeare's day; actors played on a bare stage. There was no lighting, and the actors performed on a stage with no roof in the daytime to make use of the natural light. They wore their own clothes, with just a hint of a costume (like a crown for a king), and only the props they could carry onstage with them. There was no soundtrack, although some of the plays have musical numbers in them. And most of the audience stood, talked, got drunk, talked back to the actors, and were as rowdy as people at an outdoor concert today.

So how do you get an audience like that to come to the theater and pay attention, let alone envision that it's a dark night in a castle in winter in Denmark when it's really three o'clock in the afternoon in a crowded theater on a sunny day in London? Words. The most enchanting, passionate, rousing, engaging, hilarious, painful, sweet, cruel words they had ever heard. And Shakespeare knew how to pack the house. He could write words that would still a drunken crowd so you could hear a pin drop as the actor onstage hypnotized them with his lines. The words were so important that people called it going to "hear" a play, the way we say we go to "see" a movie.

Four hundred years later, we still can't get those amazing words out of our heads. We quote him constantly, we have turned some of his images into everyday slang, and his plays are performed all over the world in record numbers. He writes more Hollywood movies than anyone. And most actors dream of getting the chance, just once, to say those words.

But not you? Have you just been trying to figure out what all this acting stuff is *about*, and now they want you to do a monologue from one of the "most challenging plays of all time"? Or do you dream of doing Shakespeare, *someday*, but thought you had a lot of training ahead of you before you were ready?

Not to worry — this idea that it's "so hard" is just a myth! It started because performing Shakespeare is a specialty of acting. Only advanced college and conservatory programs teach the technique used in performing Shakespeare, and then only at the most advanced levels, and most people have never learned it. But you're not even *in* college yet, and your teacher is assigning you Shakespeare, or you're auditioning for a show before you've gotten to those advanced classes.

So let's cut through all that and tell you what you need to know now. There are four things to know to do a Shakespearean speech: the *language,* the *words,* the *verse,* and the *structure of the speeches.*

THE LANGUAGE

Still thou mistakest, or else committest thy knaveries willfully.
— *A Midsummer Night's Dream*

What? What the heck is all that? Relax, it's just four-hundred-year-old English. Have you ever taken another language, like French or Spanish? Remember the pronoun you use for second person informal ("you" when used with friends or family)? It's *tu* in both languages. In English, it used to be *thou.* English speakers just dropped this along the way.

INFORMAL	ROYAL	FORMAL/ INFORMAL	INFORMAL	FORMAL	INFORMAL
SINGULAR	SINGULAR	PLURAL	SINGULAR	SINGULAR	PLURAL
I	we	we	thou	you	you
me	us	us	thee	you	you
my	our	our	thy	your	your
mine	ours	ours	thine	yours	yours

- The royal pronouns are only used by . . . you guessed it, royalty!

- Formal is for the same people you would call "sir" or "ma'am" (because they are older, in positions of authority, of a higher class, etc.). Can also be used to be sarcastic or distant, like saying "Yes, *ma'am!*" to your best friend when she's being bossy.

- Informal is for peers, people who are younger than you and for people of a lower class. It's also used for family members, but remember, just as there are times when you need to call your parents "ma'am" or "sir," sometimes you might use the formal for family members that are older than you.

- Note that *you* is also the informal plural, so a crowd of your friends would be *you*. This is also how it is in other languages like French. In modern day we keep trying to create a special plural, with northern Americans saying things like "you guys" and southerners saying "y'all."

- Whether your character uses *thou* or *you* in your speech is really important, especially if it switches back and forth. It shows how you feel about the person that you're speaking to, and if it changes, it shows that your feeling about that person is changing, too.

There also used to be different verb conjugations four hundred years ago:

TO MAKE	Informal, Singular	Formal and/or Plural
1st person	I make	we make
2nd person	thou makest	you make
3rd person	he/she/it maketh	they make

TO BE	Informal, Singular	Formal and/or Plural
1st person	I am	we are
2nd person	thou art	you are
3rd person	he/she/it is	they are

TO DO	Informal, Singular	Formal and/or Plural
1st person	I do	we do
2nd person	thou dost	you do
3rd person	he/she/it doth	they do

So the quote we started with translates into "Still you mistake, or else commit your knaveries willfully." When you look up this quote, you'll see the verbs are actually written as *mistak'st* and *commit'st*. This works just like contractions today: *it's* for *it is*. And just like in modern language, you make the contracted part one syllable: "mis-*taykst*" and "com-*mitst*."

There are many contractions in Shakespeare. Because the number of syllables is important to the blank verse style of the lines, Shakespeare makes crazy contractions. The best way to understand them is to use common sense. What vowel might be missing? When you pronounce the contraction and say it really fast, what does it sound like? *T'market* is "to market"; *giv'n* is "given," and so forth. If you have ever heard old songs or church hymns, this may seem familiar. When a two-syllable word gets one note, the singer sings it as a contraction, as in "heav'n." Don't spread the contraction back out and say "heaven," but say it as it's written.

Another kind of contraction is words that end in *ed*, like *stopped*. In modern day, some words pronounce the *ed* (waited), but some of them don't (turned). Four hundred years ago, *all* of them were pronounced. But if Shakespeare didn't want a particular *ed* to be pronounced because of the meter of the line, he would contract the ending, as in *stopp'd*, which is said just like *stopped* is today.

Unfortunately, these texts don't come right from the pen of Shakespeare. We don't have any of his original writings. Most of the plays weren't published in his lifetime, because if they had been, other theaters would have started performing them and that would have helped the competition. Instead, various people, including the actors, transcribed these plays. Editors came along afterward and added the stage directions, punctuation, and structure, and they broke the plays down into five acts.

So you really can't trust most of what you see besides the words themselves (which we are sure are right because most of them are the same in different versions; some books will tell you what other versions have for certain words), and you certainly can't trust the punctuation, not even for those darned contractions. When we talk about the verse, you'll see how to reason it out, but for now remember this: Start by pronouncing every *ed* you see, and pronounce all contractions as they are written.

THE WORDS

The words in Shakespeare's plays have two properties: the *sound* and the *meaning*, which often work together to create an image.

When performing Shakespeare, it's critical that you warm up your mouth first. Stretch out your lips, tongue, and jaw like you would stretch your legs before a race. You'll need to be fully relaxed and ready to properly articulate the words. Not only do you need to articulate clearly so that the audience can understand you, but since the sounds of the words are so important, you need to savor each and every sound given to you by those words. Really chew the words, hitting every consonant, drawing out the vowels, and exploring the sounds. *Over*articulate while you are rehearsing alone, and see what the sounds tell you, what images and feelings they conjure up.

Many words sound like what they mean (*onomatopoeia*) like *pop* or *splash*, so making the full sound of the word helps clarify the meaning of the word. *Alliteration*, or the repetition of sounds, also shows the character's feelings or intensifies an image. When Richard III calls himself "subtle, false, and treacherous," the *s* sounds create a serpentine quality, as Richard delights in his evil and perhaps throws a shiver through the audience. The sounds open up doors and questions that you can answer with choices about your character and speech. While you're performing, you won't need to overarticulate, but you will need to *extra*-articulate to give the sounds their due.

Extra-articulating the words also dictates the "speed limit" of how fast you speak. See how fast you can go and still savor the words. Some lines will be easy and seem to pick up speed, while others will make you slam on the brakes. Try this spell that Oberon casts on Titania in *A Midsummer Night's Dream*:

> *What thou see'st when thou dost wake*
> *Do it for thy true love take*
> *Love and languish for his sake*
> *Be it on ounce or cat or bear*
> *Pard or boar with bristled hair*
> *In thine eyes what shall appear*
> *When thou wak'st, it is thy dear.*
> *Wake when some vile thing is near.*

It starts out slowly, because you have to pick your way through all those tricky hissy and sharp consonants (*wh, t, s, st,* and *k*). Then it starts to pick up speed as you lose the hiss but keep the sharp *t* and *k* and add long vowels. "Love and languish," when extra-articulated, come out dripping with sarcasm, and this line too ends in a spiteful *k*. It hits a downhill slalom for the next three lines, gaining speed with the round *b*'s and *r*'s rolling you along. Suddenly, all those tricky consonants are back, and you come to a screeching halt on "When thou wak'st it is thy dear." If you tried to say that at the speed you were going in the previous lines, you'd sprain your tongue! The last line is its own sentence, almost like an afterthought, and spitting the *k* in *wake* and savoring the long vowel of *vile* tosses a last nasty bit into the spell.

It is just as critical to *understand* each and every word that you're saying. The only way you can create a real character who is really communicating, not just talking to hear himself talk, is to be very specific about the meaning of every word and every line. You will probably need to look a lot of the words up; some of them in special Shakespeare dictionaries or annotated editions, but some strange-sounding words are still in modern dictionaries. If, after research, you still can't tell exactly what it means, make up a meaning that fits with the context of the line and be specific about *that*. If you can't find a book to tell you that *pard* in Oberon's line means "leopard," for example, you know from the context that it must be some kind of vicious animal, so pick one and pretend that's a "pard." The whole text must mean something to *you* — or it will come out in your voice as a signal to the audience, "This isn't important, feel free not to listen."

Words have connotations too, so look not only at what a word means, but at what it *implies*. What is the difference between "she walked out of the room," and "she marched out of the room"? The word *march* means roughly "to walk," but it means more than that; it implies walking with purpose, perhaps that she's stomping her feet, and since it is a military term, it also implies toughness or strictness. Again, more questions: "Why does my character use *march* instead of *walk*? What does that say about the *way* she walked out? Why does he describe it that way?" All the words in Shakespeare's text are chosen carefully, and there are often several layers to the words in your lines.

Remember that your words are also creating the set — if your speech talks about how dark and cold it is, your audience needs to *feel* the dark and the cold even when you are giving your speech under the fluorescent lights of a warm classroom. Don't throw these images away, but savor them and use them to paint the picture for your listeners.

One of Shakespeare's favorite word tricks was *antithesis*, or two contrasting ideas next to one another. This comes up a lot in the speeches, as characters wrestle between conflicting ideas or desires. "To be or not to be" is the most famous antithesis, and the most obvious: There are two clear contrasting ideas to choose from. Some antitheses are subtler, with two or more unlikely images set against each other: "Others, like soldiers, armed in their stings/Make boot upon the summer's velvet buds," (*Henry V*). In this image, the tough soldiers with their heavy boots crush the "velvet" flowers in the fields as they march, setting the cruelty of the army against the sweetness of nature in bloom.

Each set of contrasting words, images, or ideas is important, and each part of the set must be delivered differently — making the army sound tough and the flowers sound delicate, for example. Look again at the sounds of the words — extra-articulating the word "boot" sounds heavy, and stretching out *v* and *l* in "velvet" sounds soft. Study every antithesis you find in your speech and find a way to dish up each unique image to share the contrast with your audience.

THE VERSE

Iambic pentameter is the kind of blank verse poetry that Shakespeare used in his plays. Not all of his text is in verse because it's used in the plays for high-class people and formal situations, but since most of the plays are about high-class people in formal situations, a lot of it *is* in verse. You can recognize verse because it looks like poetry, with the first letter of each line capitalized and the lines not going all the way to the end of the margin. *Prose* is text not in verse, and it looks like regular paragraphs like the one you're reading now.

Iambic pentameter has five pairs of unstressed-stressed beats ("da-DUM") per line. Most of the verse will work this way, but the actor is looking for the lines that do *not* fit the pattern, because where the meter breaks is where the acting choices have to be made.

To sort this out, mark each syllable of your text like this:

∪ = unstressed syllable   / = stressed syllable

∪ / ∪ / ∪ / ∪ / ∪ /
Now is the win- ter of our dis- con- tent

You'll know if it's working if the natural stress of the words fits the pattern; for example, for "discontent" you don't say, "dis-CON-tent," you say, "DIS-con-TENT," and that's the way it works out in the meter too. Use common sense, while keeping in mind that *sometimes* Shakespeare intentionally changed the natural stress of the words to suit his meaning or his meter.

The words are often out of order so that the stress falls on the right words. The line above should be "The winter of our discontent is now . . ." to be grammatically correct. This fits the meter, but the stress would land on *now* instead of *is*. In order to put the stress on *is*, Shakespeare turned the grammar on its head. Look at the words that get the stress in your lines. Why do those words get the stress and not others? (Why *now* and not *is*?)

If the line doesn't fit the meter perfectly (there are too many or too few syllables), put a star in the margin and keep going until you have all the lines marked that you can.

Go back to the starred lines and try to *make* them fit the meter. Sometimes a word has more than one pronunciation; *differently* can be pronounced "diff-rent-ly" or "diff-er-ent-ly," so you can add or remove a syllable just by changing how you say it. Shakespeare sometimes mangled words to fit the meter, especially proper names: *Iago* may be "Ee-ah-go" or "Ya-go," and it may be said two different ways in the same line. Two vowel sounds together may slide into each other (elision): "I am" might scan better as "I'm." You may be able to turn some of the broken lines into regular meter this way.

Now that you know which lines are definitely broken, look at what's wrong with them. Each type of break with the meter gives the actor a different kind of direction. Here are the terms and their descriptions, what they mean and what you should do about them.

Short Line: *There are less than ten beats.*

You must pause the remaining beats. Typically the pause comes after the short line, filling in the last remaining beats, but you may choose to put the pause before the line so long as you hold to the meter. You should pause approximately the number of beats that are missing in the line. You don't actually have to count beats in your head, just estimate: two beats, short pause; four to six beats, medium pause; seven to nine beats, long pause. The reason for the pause is up to the actor.

Shared Lines: *The line is short,* and *either the line before it or the line after it is also short, and the latter line is indented.*

In these lines, you and someone else *share* the meter of the line. You must say the line together; for example, if your partner begins with six beats you must come right in and finish the line with the remaining four beats so that it retains the meter it would have if it were all one line. Do not pause, but find a justification to jump right in.

Feminine Ending: *There are eleven beats, ten in the right meter and one extra* unstressed *syllable hanging off the end of the line.*

The ending has an hanging, unfinished sound. It indicates strong emotion or getting "caught" on a word: lost in thought, struck by a new idea, wishing you could take back what you just said, and so on. Definite turn on the route! Look at the last word or the last two words and see if they hold a special meaning for your character. The unstressed syllable at the end of the line is a good indicator of a pause; try it and see if it works.

Monosyllabic Line: *There are ten beats and all of them are one-syllable words.*

These lines could just be in plain iambic pentameter, but try it with *all* the syllables being stress beats, emphasizing each word individually. Since only monosyllabic lines can do this whenever there is one, you should try it. This is also true of lines where *many* of the words are one-syllable words, but not all of them.

Masculine Beginning: *There are eleven beats, ten in the right meter and one extra* stressed *beat at the beginning of the line. Or, more commonly, there are ten beats that could be in the right meter but the natural stress of the words in the first pair of beats is either a stressed-unstressed or two stresses, and it sounds wrong to force it into the stressed-unstressed pattern.*

The stress of this downbeat at the beginning is extremely important, and it is usually the hardest stress in the line. Masculine beginnings are hard to describe, but you'll know them when you find them because try as you might it just sounds too weird to say it with the right meter. It's often words like *O!* or *Ha!* or *What?* Study the word and decide why it gets such special attention. Also, the first line of each *play* has a masculine beginning, so the actor can get the audience's attention. This can also be tried for the first line of an act or scene.

Iambic Hexameter: *There are twelve beats, six pairs of "da-DUM."*

Indicates a complete running off at the mouth, and sometimes madness. It has some of the same characteristics as a feminine ending, but unlike a feminine ending's unfinished thought, this line gets all the way out before you have any idea what you've said, if you even care.

Special Meter: *There's a whole other rhythm here, and it repeats in several other lines the character has.*

1. Heightened language spoken by regular people for a special purpose, as in the lines for a play within the play like in *Midsummer* or *Hamlet*, or a poem like the love poetry in *As You Like It*. This will usually be really obvious, with different margin styles.

2. Heightened language spoken by special characters, like fairies, perhaps for a special purpose, such as casting spells. May be harder to discover. Look for it to repeat in other lines to reaffirm that you've discovered a special rhythm.

Note that a line may have more than one problem. For example, you may share a line with someone, and that combined line has a feminine ending. If your speech begins or ends with a shared line, treat it like a short line, since there won't be anyone else to share the meter with you.

If the meter is perfect in nearly every line, then your character is calm, ordered, and rational. If most of the lines have broken meter, your character is upset, disordered, and irrational, possibly insane or grief-stricken. (If the speech fits the meter, but what you're saying is clearly crazy, then rest assured that it makes perfect sense to your character!)

The directions leave you not with answers, but with *questions*. "Why does my character pause here?" "Why do I interrupt him?" "Why am I slowly stressing each word?" "What's so important about that word that it gets the stress?" "Why am I stressing that word and not this one?" "Why am I so upset?" "Why am I so calm?" All these are choices that you must make for yourself. Studying the meter is the first step to understanding your character: how he speaks and what he feels, the structure of the speech and how to deliver it.

The meter also gives direction on phrasing and where to breathe. Not all actors use the same "rules of the road" for breathing and phrasing, but here's a way that is widely accepted and easy to start with:

- You may only take a breath or a short pause at the *end* of the verse line. If the period at the end of your sentence (the *caesura*, which is sometimes a period but can also be a semicolon or colon) comes in the middle of the verse line, then you must immediately launch into the next sentence without a pause or breath. It should still sound like two sentences by your inflection, but also as thoughts rushing out, one on top of another.

- Most of the time you *won't* breathe or pause at the end of the verse line, but it's the only time you *can*. Otherwise, you would break up the meter. You will choose where you do pause and breathe as you rehearse, based on how the line is punctuated and when you will need air.

- Only come to a full stop and take a lengthy pause on lines where the *caesura* comes at the end of the verse line.

Choose your pauses based on the last word in the metered line and the first word of the next line. Once again, this leaves you with questions rather than answers. Would a pause help to deliver the weight and importance of that word by letting it sink in for a second? Or has as the word stopped your character in mid-thought because it surprised her to think of it? Or would it help the sense of your whole thought to just keep going into the next line? Does the next line start a new thought (so you might want to pause briefly before going into it)?

We often pause in the middle of sentences when we're speaking as we form the next thought. Shakespeare's verse lines often reflect this natural speech pattern, so use the built-in phrasing and see if it helps make the lines sound more natural. Phrasing and breathing are choices you make during rehearsals, but once you are into performance, you just drive, following your choices without thinking about the verse, only the intention behind your choice.

If the caesuras are at the end of verse lines, then your character feels quite comfortable that no one is going to try to interrupt her or stop her from speaking, and she feels that she has all the time in the world. If the caesuras happen inside the verse lines, so that the verse tells you to go right into the next sentence without stopping, your character may feel that someone will stop her from speaking, or her thoughts are coming out in one huge rush.

The most important thing to remember about verse: After you use the meter to find questions and make choices, forget about the verse and *play the choices*. If someone said to you after a performance, "I loved how you made all the thoughts rush together. Tell me why you did that." You would say, "My character was afraid if she stopped talking the trial would be over," not "Because all of the caesuras came in the middle of the line." The verse is there to help you make choices and create moments, not to take over your speech.

If you choose to break the meter, try to use another rule to do it. For example, in the line "Now is the winter of our discontent," the stress falls on *is*, but since *now* is the first word of the play, you could choose that rule instead and put the stress on *now*. Whether you choose to follow the meter or not is up to you, but following the verse is usually the smoothest way. If you fight against it, it can cause you more trouble by making the lines hard to say. In fact, if you find that there are one or two lines that always seem hard to get out, look at the verse again: You may have missed something, which is causing the snag.

THE SPEECHES

Now that you know how to handle the verse, you're ready to "drive" your speech. Speeches have their own structure and purpose. There are two kinds of speeches: *dialogue speeches* that come up within a scene, where one character is speaking directly to one or more persons onstage, and *soliloquies*, where the actor is alone onstage. In films, soliloquies are usually the character talking to him- or herself, soliloquies onstage are "direct address," that is, talking straight to the audience. Soliloquies offer the character a chance to reveal his or her true feelings, which is why they are so often used by villains — the villains lie so much to the other characters onstage that without direct address, the audience would never know what to believe. Lovers use them to show us their true feelings too, though they might deny them when talking to other characters.

In either case, the structure of the speech is very similar. There are three parts to a speech:

1. *The Opening:* reacting to the current situation — perhaps laying out a problem that must be solved, or emotions that need to be resolved — or to something someone has said.

2. *The Argument:* looking at the situation from different sides — perhaps looking for solutions or causes of a problem, or analyzing emotions — or explaining your stated position to someone by giving examples.

3. *The Resolution:* coming to a decision of what you will do next, or what you want someone else to do next, or even deciding there's nothing to be done.

Sounds like papers for school, doesn't it? First state the premise, then back it up with examples, and then restate the theme in your conclusion. The difference is, in the speeches the conclusion is not always the same as the original premise, as the character often comes to a different conclusion after considering the argument.

These three apply to all kinds of speeches, including cursing, joking, and narration. Cursing has "I hate you"; "Here's why"; and "Here's what I hope happens to you." Jokes and analogies ("All the world's a stage") have the opening, middle, and punch line like jokes do today. Narration like those of the Chorus in *Henry V* is another kind of soliloquy, and it also has three parts, "Welcome," or "Now our play changes time/location"; "Here's what's happening now," (setting the scene); and "Here's what's about to happen," or "Let's watch . . ."

The most important rule of speeches is to not allow it to be all one emotion or mood. Don't play a "summary" of the speech by deciding, "This is where she decides she's leaving town and she's sad" and just playing "sad about leaving" the whole time. If she gives three things she'll miss about home in the argument section, play each one differently. They each mean something different to her, so show us that. Or she may display several emotions and be torn between being sad about leaving and excited about the journey.

Speeches are a journey of exploration, and you need to play each thought for itself. You must *share* this journey with audience members, be their tour guide and make them feel every image and emotion along with you. Use the power of the speech to throw your energy outward and catch all your listeners in it like a net.

When you choose a speech, pick one whose story really speaks to you. Find one that, when you read it, you think, "Oh, yeah, that's it, you are so right!" Discover what it is about the speech that speaks to you, and share that with the audience. Picking a speech whose story you really want to tell is half the battle. Use it to say what you feel in your own heart. Helena has a couple of speeches in *A Midsummer Night's Dream* about loneliness and low self-esteem — the boy she likes has just fallen in love with her best friend who is petite and cute and already has a great boyfriend. She, on the other hand, is really tall and calls herself "ugly as a bear," wondering why everything is so easy for her friend and so hard for her.

Do you sometimes feel like that on a low day? Have you ever liked someone who liked your friend instead? Doesn't it sometimes feel like *everyone* has a boyfriend or girlfriend, the perfect romance, but not you? Hopefully you don't feel this way very often, but if you can relate to it, then this can be your chance to say what you feel but use Helena's words. Your connection to it makes it come alive for the audience right off the bat. It could be argued that the art of acting is the art of finding a speech that doesn't speak to you at all, but still being able to play it as if it did — and you'll work up to that skill level. For now, there are 111 speeches in this book, and there is no doubt that one of them is playing your song.

That was a lot of information, but all together this technique can make Shakespeare easier to perform than modern theater. It's easier to memorize verse because of the meter (just as it's easier to learn song lyrics than a paragraph). In modern plays you have to decide for yourself how to phrase a line or which words to stress, but Shakespearean plays are laid out like a blueprint, giving you a map to performing the text.

Learning how to perform Shakespeare actually trains you for modern plays, too, because you will habitually study the words for which words are used and how they sound, and you'll be primed to dissect the text in a way that other, less trained actors don't.

BASIC ACTING BY THE BARD

In *Hamlet*, a troupe of actors arrives and Hamlet invites them to perform. He asks that the players take a well-known play and change the story, so that he can trap his uncle into confessing to murdering Hamlet's father. (He changes the play into a re-enactment of the murder.) A true performance is critical to Hamlet, as his plan will only work if the performance is realistic, understandable, and gripping. After rewriting the play, he meets with the actors to give them a few pointers on acting.

And so it is our great fortune that we have acting lessons straight from William Shakespeare himself, in the form of this speech, commonly known as "Hamlet's Speech to the Players."

Let's take a look at what Shakespeare has to say. I'll take one piece of advice at a time, and talk about what it means and how to use it.

Speak the speech, I pray you, as I pronounced it to you, trip-pingly on the tongue;

This is the First Golden Rule of Shakespearean Acting: You *must articulate.*

The most important word in this line is *trippingly.* This means, according to *The Yale Shakespeare,* "rapidly but with neat articulation." It's critical to warm up your voice and your mouth before you try to deliver Shakespeare, and it's equally critical that you say the words crisply and cleanly.

". . . as I pronounced it to you," is a reference to the new lines that he's given them in the play. But it also refers to the way Shakespeare used the meter to give the words a rhythm, and the way actors can use that meter to figure out how to deliver the lines, which is known as *scansion technique.* "Do it the way I wrote it," he's saying.

but if you mouth it, as many of our players do, I'd as lief the town crier spoke my lines.

Here the key is *mouth,* which *The Yale Shakespeare* says means "to speak loudly with false emphasis and indistinctness." Today we call this "hamming it up." A lot of people think that's all Shakespearean performances are, just a bunch of ham actors bellowing out lines in falsely deep voices with no regard to what the lines actually mean. But that's not at all what Shakespeare's about! He says here that if you're going to do that, he'd rather a cable channel news anchor played the part.

Nor do not saw the air too much with your hand, thus, but use all gently, for in the very torrent, tempest, and (as I may say) the whirlwind of your passion you must acquire and beget a temperance that may give it smoothness.

This goes to the heart of gesturing. Nowadays when a ham starts thrashing about onstage so that his gestures, mannerisms, and actions are as silly as his voice, we call that "chewing the scenery." You need to move naturally, the way people do in real life.

Shakespeare also acknowledges that sometimes when you're acting you'll start to get carried away with yourself and get "caught up in the part." That's natural, but you just have to make sure that you keep control of your physical movements and your voice so that they're natural too. This way, instead of your character being a rough sketch, it will be smooth and natural, like a real person.

O it offends me to the soul to hear a robustious periwig-pated fellow tear a passion to tatters, to very rags, to split the ears of the groundlings, who for the most part are capable of nothing but inexplicable dumb-shows and noise. I would have such a fellow whipped . . .

This line talks about how awful it is to see the aforementioned bad acting habits all rolled into one performance.

Be not too tame, neither, but let your own discretion be your tutor.

To "be too tame" means to be too quiet or still onstage. One of the first rules of acting is: No matter what you're doing, if the audience can't tell, it doesn't count. This can sometimes come in handy if you have to sneak a prop out of your pocket or whisper to another actor that the couch onstage is about to fall apart. But if what you're doing is part of the play, you have to make sure the audience sees, hears, and feels what you're doing. They have to hear your lines; they have to see your gestures, movements, and facial expressions; and they have to understand by watching you what is going on with your character at every moment.

What if you're *supposed* to be still? Think about why you would be still. Maybe your character is in shock, or trying not to be seen by another character onstage. Think about what's going on with your character, and what the underlying meaning to your actions is. The underlying meaning, known as *subtext*, has to come across to the audience in your stillness. They should be able to tell the difference between standing still in shock, standing still in order not to be noticed, and standing still because you're "too tame."

The rest of the time, remember: *You're onstage.* How far away is the audience? How big is the theater? Are you wearing a body mike?

How quiet can you be and still be heard? (Or, how loud can you get if needed without getting feedback on your body mike?) How far do you have to move your hand in a gesture so that the people in the back can tell that you did it? How big do your facial expressions have to be so that most of the people can read your emotions?

Your facial expressions and gestures may look weird up close, and your voice may sound unnaturally loud, but if the audience isn't going to *be* up close, then that's fine. Figure out how big you must be (or, in the case of a small, intimate theater space, how small you must be) and consider that as your new level of reality. Then create a character that seems real at *that level* of reality.

Most of all, don't be afraid. Don't be timid. Do everything you do deliberately and with complete conviction. It's only what you do halfway that looks dumb onstage.

Suit the action to the word, the word to the action . . .

This is the second Golden Rule of Shakespearean acting: Use only those movements and physical actions that punctuate and help clarify the words that you're saying, and only move when you have words to move you.

In Shakespearean performance more than in any other kind, the words are all that matter — they are the whole universe of the play. In modern day we see a play or a movie, but in Shakespeare's day they heard a play. Everything that happens onstage must serve the words, and that includes your actions and gestures.

This gives rise to another basic tenet of stage acting, don't make large movements (like walking) unless it's your line. Small movements like eating or drinking are fine, but any large movement while someone else is speaking distracts the audience's attention away from the person who is speaking. Save your movement for *your* next line. Of course, sometimes the director will tell you to move on someone else's line, when you are moving in direct answer to what they are saying. In that case, you are suiting *your* action to *their* words.

. . . with this special observance, that you o'erstep not the modesty of nature, for anything so overdone is from the pur-

*pose of playing, whose end, both at the first and now, was
and is to hold, as 'twere, the mirror up to nature, to show
virtue her own feature, scorn her own image, and the very
age and body of the time his form and pressure.*

This goes to the heart of why we do theater in the first place.
What is the point of putting on a play, film, or TV show?

What is the one thing that we all have in common? Life. We all
feel the same basic emotions, even if we feel them for different reasons. We all have to face basically the same society and its rules and
customs. We all have strengths and dreams, and we all have flaws
and fears. We all make mistakes. We all fall in love. Some of us lose
that love; most are separated from it at one point or another. Most
of us grew up with parents. Most of us have, or will have, children.
We were all once children. We all have obstacles. We all have to answer to someone. We all want things. We all struggle against obstacles.
We all wonder why we're here, and what the purpose of life is.

This is the essence of telling stories through acting, whether it's
on stage, film, or TV: to help us all understand the life we're living
by looking at situations that any of us could be in and watching
other people go through it. The story itself usually ends with a judgment about how things should be, how people should act, or the way
a situation should be handled. The more simple a show, like a children's TV show, the clearer the judgment will be. There are good
guys and bad guys, and there will be a moral at the end. The more
sophisticated a story, like *Hamlet* or *The Godfather*, the more that is
left up to the audience to decide what is right and what is wrong and
which characters they are going to support.

Specifically, Shakespeare says "the purpose of playing" is:

- *to hold, as 'twere, the mirror up to nature.* To show life as
  it really is, and to try to understand it, and the people in it.

- *to show virtue her own feature.* To hold up examples of
  goodness; to understand what it means to do good and
  noble things.

- *[to show] scorn, her own image.* To show examples of the

ways that people are cruel to each other; to understand the effect of those actions.

- *and [to show] the age and body of the time his form and pressure.* To show what it's like to live in this day and age, or to show what it was like in times past, or to comment on how things are today by showing how things might be in the future.

Keep in mind that Shakespeare never saw the strange world of absurdist theater or science-fiction movies. But even these genres are ways of taking the essential struggles that we all face and holding a mirror up to them, not by showing them exactly as they are, but in such a way that we can step back and see them objectively. The exotic environments, mythologies, and characters of those stories are so foreign to us that we can see the conflict, actions, and characters by getting away from our preconceptions and into a symbolic setting. Shakespeare did this by telling us stories of fairies and wizards, as well as stories of kings and queens, as this was just as distant from the common man.

Now this overdone, or come tardy off, though it makes the unskillful laugh, cannot but make the judicious grieve, the censure of the which one must in your allowance o'erweigh a whole theater of others. O, there be players that I have seen play and heard others praise, and that highly (not to speak it profanely) that, neither having the accent of Christians nor the gait of a Christian, pagan, nor man, have so strutted and bellowed that I have thought some of nature's journeymen had made men and not made them well, they imitated humanity so abominably.

Let's start with a note about this "Christian" business. Back in Shakespeare's time, the Christian churches controlled all the European countries. Not everyone who lived in Europe was a Christian, but it was the official religion. For the most part, all the European cultures, customs, fashions, and governments were the same. But outside Europe travelers found strange, exotic cultures (as in Africa, the Middle East, and the Far East) that were very different from what they knew at home. So it was common to say "Christian" when you meant European, or "civilized," or "the way things are done." "Pagan" just means "foreigners."

The other part of this line that needs explanation is the "nature's journeyman" bit. A journeyman is an apprentice, sort of like a college intern. So to say that it seems that men are made by nature's journeymen is to say, "It's like God made everything else but when it came time to make man, he turned it over to an intern to do, it was done so badly."

OK, so what's the acting lesson here? Shakespeare has been saying that you should create a realistic, natural character. The translation for this instruction is there are actors out there that when they're acting don't speak or walk like "normal" people, or even foreign people, or like people at *all*.

You *should* create an original character. Each person in real life is different, like snowflakes, and you want the character you're playing to seem real, so it's good to create a person like no one's ever seen. But the character still has to seem like a *person*, even if he's a unique person. (OK, unless you're playing an animal or a fairy or something, we're assuming here that you are actually playing a person.)

The key words in this line are "imitated humanity." That is, you need to imitate a real human being to create a character. He or she may be someone you made up, or based on a real person, but either way *he or she must seem like a real person.*

> And let those that play your clowns speak no more than is
> set down for them, for there be of them that will themselves
> laugh, to set on some quantity of barren spectators to laugh
> too, though in the mean time some necessary question of the
> play be then to be considered. That's villainous, and shows
> a most pitiful ambition in the fool that uses it.

You won't see much ad-libbing in Shakespeare: Try making up some Shakespearean-sounding lines off the top of your head and see how it goes! But there is such a thing as physical ad-libbing, which usually happens in comedies. Just as an actor doing a tragedy can be overly dramatic or "chew the scenery," an actor in a comedy could, if he got on a roll, take over the play with a comic "solo" of physical business, like playing with his food or tangling himself in his coat.

This may seem funny at the time, but does it serve the play? Is this silly comic business creating a real character that we can laugh at as he helps tell the story, or just creating a distraction from what is supposed to be the point of the play? That's what Shakespeare means when he says, " . . . there is some question of the play to be considered." This is true of all acting, comedy or tragedy. You may know the saying, "If you're not part of the solution, then you're part of the problem." In acting, if you're not helping to tell the larger picture of the story, then you're hurting the show.

Go, make you ready.

OK, I admit it, this is just a line Hamlet says to the players to get them to exit the stage. But when you're reading this separate from the play, and looking at it as acting lessons, this line says something different. Tto me, it says, "Go do your actor homework." Work on your voice and your mannerisms, create a natural character, develop your preparation for performance. Warm up. Think about how you're going to "hold the mirror up to nature" and how your character work supports the story that you're part of telling.

Go, make you ready.

Jill K. Swanson

SOME USEFUL
AUDITION TIPS

The introduction to this book gives a thorough understanding of working with the text. If you are preparing any of these monologues for audition purposes, the following is a quick and simple checklist to review as part of your rehearsal process.

It is quite common for directors to ask to see *two contrasting pieces* — one contemporary, the other classical. Less often you might be asked to show two classical pieces contrasting in tone, perhaps one comic and one serious.

Depending on the type of audition you are asked to do, you are almost always given a *time limit*. Time limits for the total audition usually range between two and five minutes. Knowing your time limit, it is wise to edit your pieces judiciously and practice often, making sure you are well within the limit. It is not uncommon to simply be cut off by a timer, which draws attention to your lack of preparation. Do yourself the favor of having total peace of mind knowing you will not be cut off because of a timing violation.

THERE IS NO SUBTEXT IN SHAKESPEARE

The text reveals the speaker's state of mind and intent in a straightforward manner. Often the physical direction is fairly explicitly implied, such as when Juliet says in Act III, Scene v of *Romeo and Juliet*: "Good father, I beseech you on my knees" and reveals her physical position and to whom she is speaking.

THE AUDITION BEGINS THE MOMENT THE AUDITORS SEE YOU

Enter the room with good posture and a performance-level energy that shows you are prepared and happy to share your work. Be sufficiently warmed up so that you are not wiggling your fingers, rolling your head, stretching, or doing anything to distract from professional poise. Take your position, stop, smile, breathe, and wait until you have the auditor's full attention. Say a simple greeting and your name and announce your pieces clearly. Timed auditions usually include your name and introduction, so be brief. There is no need to go into an elaborate description of the scene setting. Your auditors will probably be quite familiar with the text.

Which brings us to another point: Shakespeare chose every word with *a purpose as to meaning and rhythm.* This is not material that rewards ad-libs or paraphrasing. Do the Bard justice and learn the words exactly; if you need to look up words that seem archaic or unfamiliar, by all means do your homework.

Assuming you have done all that, allow yourself to relax and enjoy the moment. Trust the text and yourself!

Lisa Bansavage

USING THIS BOOK

For young actors wishing to hone their skills, this book offers a selection of age-appropriate audition material from one of the greatest monologue writers of all time, William Shakespeare (1564–1616). The characters who speak herein are either teens or young adults, and for the most part they speak of youthful things that have remained conversational topics and concerns of young people through the centuries: love and romance, pranks and jokes, boasts and demonstrations of physical prowess, and — on the darker side of the psyche — deceit, greed, and violence.

Aside from their youth orientation, these 111 monologues were chosen to span a variety of character type and tone, with lengths ranging from from fifteen seconds to two minutes flat. Twenty-nine of Shakespeare's thirty-seven plays are represented, offering a cross-section of the Bard's canon. If your favorite Shakespeare monologue is not here, despair not, gentles . . . there could yet well be more volumes of *One Hundred Eleven Shakespeare Monologues for Teens* on the way to the printer even as we speak, anon!

There are many edited versions of Shakespeare on the market and certain spellings, punctuations, and line placements vary from edition to edition. The character Phebe may appear in some editions as Phoebe, Thisby as Thisbe, and so on. There are occasional spelling and punctuation anomalies (the "woeful ballad" of which Jaques speaks in *As You Like It*, the "woful breast" cited by Joan La Pucelle in *Henry VI Part I*), but these should not stand in the way of comprehending and delivering the monologue.

We have used a venerable source for this book: *The Complete Works of William Shakespeare, The Cambridge Edition Text*, edited by William Aldis Wright. There are other popular editions — the Riverside, the Arden, the Pelican, the Folger Library, and so forth — all of which stem from the First Folio edition of Shakespeare's works published in 1623. The First Folio is the oldest available printing of Shakespeare's works and gives the closest glimpse we have of how the plays were originally performed. Scholars agree that the spellings, punctuation (or lack thereof), and other conventions used in the First Folio contain hints for actors that are absent in the later versions after various editors "improved" the original work.

The monologues in this book are organized by *gender* and then by the *genre* of the play — Comedy, History, Tragedy. A few monologues are spoken by actors of unspecified gender and may be performed by either women or men. Each monologue also possesses a particular *tone* — comic, serious, or seriocomic (a mixture of serious and comic, as when someone speaks seriously about a humorous subject). For a fuller and very enlightening discussion of Shakespeare's prose and verse *styles of text*, see the incisive introduction by Jill K. Swanson.

Basic *scene setting* information has been provided, along with a few stage directions helpful in setting the character's action or framing the scene, but, for the most part, Shakespeare was adept at providing in the character's speech all the necessary "background" information needed about the character and moment.

This sign *(* * *)* indicates that dialogue from another character or some other action or musical interlude occurs here, briefly interrupting the monologue flow; the actor should incorporate this unseen or unheard activity into the delivery. If you want to know what actually happens in that space, be sure to consult the play itself; the *act and scene locations* are provided for this purpose.

The *approximate run times* are, of course, approximate and subject to each actor's delivery; there may be occasions when an actor is required to edit the monologue for a particular audition.

Nearly four hundred years after his death, the plays of Shakespeare are still one of the best sources of audition material for modern actors. We hope this book will assist young actors in finding audition pieces that not only show their acting skills to best advantage but also help them grow in their craft under the tutelage of one of the greatest wordsmiths in the English language.

A fine volley of words, gentlemen, and quickly shot off.
— Silvia, *The Two Gentlemen of Verona*

L. E. McCullough, Ph.D.
Children's Playwriting Institute, Woodbridge, New Jersey

FEMALE
MONOLOGUES

Play: *A Midsummer Night's Dream*
Character: Helena
Genre: Comedy
Tone: Seriocomic
Style: Verse
Act/Scene: I i
Approx. Run Time: .30
Scene Setting: Helena envies her friend Hermia's qualities that attract
Demetrius, a man Helena wants to love her.

———◦———

Call you me fair? that fair again unsay.
Demetrius loves your fair: O happy fair!
Your eyes are lode-stars; and your tongue's sweet air
More tuneable than lark to shepherd's ear,
When wheat is green, when hawthorn buds appear.
Sickness is catching: O, were favour so,
Yours would I catch, fair Hermia, ere I go;
My ear should catch your voice, my eye your eye,
My tongue should catch your tongue's sweet melody.
Were the world mine, Demetrius being bated,
The rest I'ld give to be to you translated.
O, teach me how you look, and with what art
You sway the motion of Demetrius' heart.

Play: *A Midsummer Night's Dream*
Character: Helena
Genre: Comedy
Tone: Seriocomic
Style: Verse
Act/Scene: I i
Approx. Run Time: 1.00
Scene Setting: Helena knows that Demetrius, the man she loves, is in love with Hermia. When Hermia runs off with Lysander, she resolves to tell Demetrius, hoping it will endear her to him.

How happy some o'er other some can be!
Through Athens I am thought as fair as she.
But what of that? Demetrius thinks not so;
He will not know what all but he do know:
And as he errs, doting on Hermia's eyes,
So I, admiring of his qualities:
Things base and vile, holding no quantity,
Love can transpose to form and dignity:
Love looks not with the eyes, but with the mind;
And therefore is wing'd Cupid painted blind:
Nor hath Love's mind of any judgement taste;
Wings and no eyes figure unheedy haste:
And therefore is Love said to be a child,
Because in choice he is so oft beguiled.
As waggish boys in game themselves forswear,
So the boy Love is perjured everywhere:
For ere Demetrius look'd on Hermia's eyne,
He hail'd down oaths that he was only mine;
And when this hail some heat from Hermia felt,
So he dissolved, and showers of oaths did melt.
I will go tell him of fair Hermia's flight:

Then to the wood will he to-morrow night
Pursue her; and for this intelligence
If I have thanks, it is a dear expense:
But herein mean I to enrich my pain,
To have his sight thither and back again.
    (Exit.)

Play: *A Midsummer Night's Dream*
Character: Helena
Genre: Comedy
Tone: Seriocomic
Style: Verse
Act/Scene: III ii
Approx. Run Time: .40
Scene Setting: Lysander and Demetrius have both been put under spells that make them love Helena, but the more they declare their love, the more she believes her friends are deliberately mocking her.

O spite! O hell! I see you all are bent
To set against me for your merriment:
If you were civil and knew courtesy,
You would not do me thus much injury.
Can you not hate me, as I know you do,
But you must join in souls to mock me too?
If you were men, as men you are in show,
You would not use a gentle lady so;
To vow, and swear, and superpraise my parts,
When I am sure you hate me with your hearts.
You both are rivals, and love Hermia;
And now both rivals, to mock Helena:
A trim exploit, a manly enterprise,
To conjure tears up in a poor maid's eyes
With your derision! none of noble sort
Would so offend a virgin, and extort
A poor soul's patience, all to make you sport.

Play: *A Midsummer Night's Dream*
Character: Hermia
Genre: Comedy
Tone: Serious
Style: Verse
Act/Scene: II ii
Approx. Run Time: .30
Scene Setting: Hermia has suffered a nightmare and now awakens to find herself alone in the woods.

(*Awaking.*)
Help me, Lysander, help me! do thy best
To pluck this crawling serpent from my breast!
Ay me, for pity! what a dream was here!
Lysander, look how I do quake with fear:
Methought a serpent eat my heart away,
And you sat smiling at his cruel prey.
Lysander! what, removed? Lysander! lord!
What, out of hearing? gone? no sound, no word?
Alack, where are you? speak, an if you hear;
Speak, of all loves! I swoon almost with fear.
No? then I well perceive you are not nigh:
Either death or you I'll find immediately.
(*Exit.*)

Play: *A Midsummer Night's Dream*
Character: Hermia
Genre: Comedy
Tone: Seriocomic
Style: Verse
Act/Scene: III ii
Approx. Run Time: .55
Scene Setting: Hermia fears that her boyfriend Lysander's rival Demetrius has done harm to Lysander to clear the field for his own suit of Hermia.

Now I but chide; but I should use thee worse,
For thou, I fear, hast given me cause to curse,
If thou hast slain Lysander in his sleep,
Being o'er shoes in blood, plunge in the deep,
And kill me too.
The sun was not so true unto the day
As he to me: would he have stolen away
From sleeping Hermia? I'll believe as soon
This whole earth may be bored, and that the moon
May through the centre creep, and so displease
Her brother's noontide with the Antipodes.
It cannot be but thou hast murder'd him;
So should a murderer look, so dead, so grim.
    (* * *)
What's this to my Lysander? where is he?
Ah, good Demetrius, wilt thou give him me?
    (* * *)
Out, dog! out, cur! thou drivest me past the bounds
Of maiden's patience. Hast thou slain him, then?
Henceforth be never number'd among men!
O, once tell true, tell true, even for my sake!

Durst thou have look'd upon him being awake,
And hast thou kill'd him sleeping? O brave touch!
Could not a worm, an adder, do so much?
An adder did it; for with doubler tongue
Than thine, thou serpent, never adder stung.

Play: *All's Well That Ends Well*
Character: Helena
Genre: Comedy
Tone: Serious
Style: Verse
Act/Scene: I i
Approx. Run Time: .35
Scene Setting: Despite the pain of her unrequited love for Bertram, Helena resolves to do her best to heal the ailing King.

⟫•◦•⟪

Our remedies oft in ourselves do lie,
Which we ascribe to heaven: the fated sky
Gives us free scope; only doth backward pull
Our slow designs when we ourselves are dull.
What power is it which mounts my love so high;
That makes me see, and cannot feed mine eye?
The mightiest space in fortune nature brings
To join like likes and kiss like native things.
Impossible be strange attempts to those
That weigh their pains in sense, and do suppose
What hath been cannot be: who ever strove
To show her merit, that did miss her love?
The king's disease — my project may deceive me,
But my intents are fix'd, and will not leave me.
　　(Exit.)

Play: *All's Well That Ends Well*
Character: Helena
Genre: Comedy
Tone: Serious
Style: Verse
Act/Scene: I iii
Approx. Run Time: 1.00
Scene Setting: Helena tells Bertram's mother that she is in love with Bertram even though she knows that they are from different social classes.

―――――――――

Then, I confess,
Here on my knee, before high heaven and you,
That before you, and next unto high heaven,
I love your son.
My friends were poor, but honest; so's my love:
Be not offended; for it hurts not him
That he is loved of me: I follow him not
By any token of presumptuous suit;
Nor would I have him till I do deserve him;
Yet never know how that desert should be.
I know I love in vain, strive against hope;
Yet in this captious and intenible sieve
I still pour in the waters of my love,
And lack not to lose still: thus, Indian-like,
Religious in mine error, I adore
The sun, that looks upon his worshipper,
But knows of him no more. My dearest madam,
Let not your hate encounter with my love
For loving where you do: but if yourself,
Whose aged honour cites a virtuous youth,
Did ever in so true a flame of liking

Wish chastely and love dearly, that your Dian
Was both herself and love; O, then, give pity
To her, whose state is such that cannot choose
But lend and give where she is sure to lose;
That seeks not to find that her search implies,
But riddle-like lives sweetly where she dies!

Play: *As You Like It*
Character: Phebe
Genre: Comedy
Tone: Comic
Style: Verse
Act/Scene: III v
Approx. Run Time: .45
Scene Setting: Phebe is exasperated by the persistent suit of Silvius and attempts to discourage him once and for all.

———————

I would not be thy executioner:
I fly thee, for I would not injure thee.
Thou tell'st me there is murder in mine eye:
'Tis pretty, sure, and very probable,
That eyes, that are the frail'st and softest things,
Who shut their coward gates on atomies,
Should be call'd tyrants, butchers, murderers!
Now I do frown on thee with all my heart;
And if mine eyes can wound, now let them kill thee:
Now counterfeit to swoon; why now fall down;
Or if thou canst not, O, for shame, for shame,
Lie not, to say mine eyes are murderers!
Now show the wound mine eye hath made in thee:
Scratch thee but with a pin, and there remains
Some scar of it; lean but upon a rush,
The cicatrice and capable impressure
Thy palm some moment keeps; but now mine eyes,
Which I have darted at thee, hurt thee not,
Nor, I am sure, there is no force in eyes
That can do hurt.

Play: *As You Like It*
Character: Phebe
Genre: Comedy
Tone: Comic
Style: Verse
Act/Scene: III v
Approx. Run Time: 1.10
Scene Setting: Phebe has developed a crush on Rosalind (who is in disguise as a boy) and is pumping Silvius for more information about "him" while denying her true feelings.

Think not I love him, though I ask for him;
'Tis but a peevish boy; yet he talks well;
But what care I for words? yet words do well
When he that speaks them pleases those that hear.
It is a pretty youth: not very pretty:
But, sure, he's proud, and yet his pride becomes him:
He'll make a proper man: the best thing in him
Is his complexion; and faster than his tongue
Did make offence his eye did heal it up.
He is not very tall; yet for his years he's tall:
His leg is but so so; and yet 'tis well:
There was a pretty redness in his lip,
A little riper and more lusty red
Than that mix'd in his cheek; 'twas just the difference
Between the constant red and mingled damask.
There be some women, Silvius, had they mark'd him
In parcels as I did, would have gone near
To fall in love with him: but, for my part,
I love him not nor hate him not; and yet
I have more cause to hate him than to love him:
For what had he to do to chide at me?
He said mine eyes were black and my hair black;
And, now I am remember'd, scorn'd at me:

I marvel why I answer'd not again:
But that's all one; omittance is no quittance.
I'll write to him a very taunting letter,
And thou shalt bear it: wilt thou, Silvius?
    (* * *)
I'll write it straight;
The matter's in my head and in my heart:
I will be bitter with him and passing short.
Go with me, Silvius.
    (*Exit.*)

Play: *As You Like It*
Character: Rosalind
Genre: Comedy
Tone: Comic
Style: Verse
Act/Scene: III v
Approx. Run Time: 1.05
Scene Setting: Rosalind scolds Phebe for being so hard on Silvius.

————➤◦◄————

And why, I pray you? Who might be your mother,
That you insult, exult, and all at once,
Over the wretched? What though you have no beauty, —
As, by my faith, I see no more in you
Than without candle may go dark to bed —
Must you be therefore proud and pitiless?
Why, what means this? Why do you look on me?
I see no more in you than in the ordinary
Of nature's sale-work. 'Od's my little life,
I think she means to tangle my eyes too!
No, faith, proud mistress, hope not after it:
'Tis not your inky brows, your black silk hair,
Your bugle eyeballs, nor your cheek of cream,
That can entame my spirits to your worship.
You foolish shepherd, wherefore do you follow her,
Like foggy south, puffing with wind and rain?
You are a thousand times a properer man
Than she a woman: 'tis such fools as you
That makes the world full of ill-favour'd children:
'Tis not her glass, but you, that flatters her;
And out of you she sees herself more proper
Than any of her lineaments can show her.
But, mistress, know yourself: down on your knees,

And thank heaven, fasting, for a good man's love:
For I must tell you friendly in your ear,
Sell when you can: you are not for all markets:
Cry the man mercy; love him; take his offer:
Foul is most foul, being foul to be a scoffer.
So take her to thee, shepherd: fare you well.

Play: *The Comedy of Errors*
Character: Adriana
Genre: Comedy
Tone: Comic
Style: Verse
Act/Scene: II i
Approx. Run Time: .35
Scene Setting: Adriana laments her stale marriage.

His company must do his minions grace,
Whilst I at home starve for a merry look.
Hath homely age the alluring beauty took
From my poor cheek? then he hath wasted it:
Are my discourses dull? barren my wit?
If voluble and sharp discourse be marr'd,
Unkindness blunts it more than marble hard:
Do their gay vestments his affections bait?
That's not my fault: he's master of my state:
What ruins are in me that can be found,
By him not ruin'd? then is he the ground
Of my defeatures. My decayed fair
A sunny look of his would soon repair
But, too unruly deer, he breaks the pale
And feeds from home; poor I am but his stale.

Play: *The Comedy of Errors*
Character: Courtezan
Genre: Comedy
Tone: Comic
Style: Verse
Act/Scene: IV iii
Approx. Run Time: .35
Scene Setting: The Courtezan has mistaken Antipholus' twin for her customer; she wonders at his denial that he owes her a ring and necklace and decides to go to his wife.

Now, out of doubt Antipholus is mad,
Else would he never so demean himself.
A ring he hath of mine worth forty ducats,
And for the same he promised me a chain:
Both one and other he denies me now.
The reason that I gather he is mad,
Besides this present instance of his rage,
Is a mad tale he told to-day at dinner,
Of his own doors being shut against his entrance.
Belike his wife, acquainted with his fits,
On purpose shut the doors against his way.
My way is now to hie home to his house,
And tell his wife that, being lunatic,
He rush'd into my house and took perforce
My ring away. This course I fittest choose;
For forty ducats is too much to lose.
    (Exit.)

Play: *The Comedy of Errors*
Character: Luciana
Genre: Comedy
Tone: Comic
Style: Verse
Act/Scene: III ii
Approx. Run Time: 1.00
Scene Setting: Luciana scolds her brother-in-law for his ill treatment of his wife.

———◦———

And may it be that you have quite forgot
A husband's office? shall, Antipholus,
Even in the spring of love, thy love-springs rot?
Shall love, in building, grow so ruinous?
If you did wed my sister for her wealth,
Then for her wealth's sake use her with more kindness:
Or if you like elsewhere, do it by stealth;
Muffle your false love with some show of blindness:
Let not my sister read it in your eye;
Be not thy tongue thy own shame's orator;
Look sweet, be fair, become disloyalty;
Apparel vice like virtue's harbinger;
Bear a fair presence, though your heart be tainted;
Teach sin the carriage of a holy saint;
Be secret-false: what need she be acquainted?
What simple thief brags of his own attaint?
'Tis double wrong, to truant with your bed
And let her read it in thy looks at board:
Shame hath a bastard fame, well managed;
Ill deeds are doubled with an evil word.
Alas, poor women! make us but believe,
Being compact of credit, that you love us;

Though others have the arm, show us the sleeve;
We in your motion turn and you may move us.
Then, gentle brother, get you in again;
Comfort my sister, cheer her, call her wife
'Tis holy sport, to be a little vain,
When the sweet breath of flattery conquers strife.

Play: *Cymbeline*
Character: Imogen
Genre: Comedy
Tone: Comic
Style: Verse
Act/Scene: I vi
Approx. Run Time: .35
Scene Setting: Imogen spurns the advances of a stranger while her husband is away and calls to her husband's servant, Pisanio, for help.

———⟫·◦·⟪———

Away! I do condemn mine ears that have
So long attended thee. If thou wert honourable,
Thou wouldst have told this tale for virtue, not
For such an end thou seek'st, as base as strange.
Thou wrong'st a gentleman who is as far
From thy report as thou from honour, and
Solicit'st here a lady that disdains
Thee and the devil alike. What ho, Pisanio!
The king my father shall be made acquainted
Of thy assault: if he shall think it fit,
A saucy stranger in his court to mart
As in a Romish stew, and to expound
His beastly mind to us, he hath a court
He little cares for, and a daughter who
He not respects at all. What, ho, Pisanio!

Play: *Cymbeline*
Character: Imogen
Genre: Comedy
Tone: Serious
Style: Verse
Act/Scene: III iv
Approx. Run Time: .30
Scene Setting: Imogen protests her innocence to Pisanio after he shows her a letter from her husband instructing Pisanio to kill her for her alleged infidelity.

———⇒»·०·«⇐———

I false! Thy conscience witness: Iachimo,
Thou didst accuse him of incontinency;
Thou then look'dst like a villain; now methinks
Thy favour's good enough. Some jay of Italy,
Whose mother was her painting, hath betray'd him:
Poor I am stale, a garment out of fashion;
And, for I am richer than to hang by the walls,
I must be ripp'd: — to pieces with me! — O,
Men's vows are women's traitors! All good seeming,
By thy revolt, O husband, shall be thought
Put on for villany; not born where't grows,
But worn a bait for ladies.

Play: *Love's Labour's Lost*
Character: Princess
Genre: Comedy
Tone: Comic
Style: Verse
Act/Scene: II i
Approx. Run Time: .50
Scene Setting: The Princess of France asks Lord Boyet to find out if Navarre has an interest in her.

———➤•◗•◖———

Good Lord Boyet, my beauty, though but mean,
Needs not the painted flourish of your praise:
Beauty is bought by judgement of the eye,
Not utter'd by base sale of chapmen's tongues:
I am less proud to hear you tell my worth
Than you much willing to be counted wise
In spending your wit in the praise of mine.
But now to task the tasker: good Boyet,
You are not ignorant, all-telling fame
Doth noise abroad, Navarre hath made a vow,
Till painful study shall outwear three years,
No woman may approach his silent court:
Therefore to's seemeth it a needful course,
Before we enter his forbidden gates,
To know his pleasure; and in that behalf,
Bold of your worthiness, we single you
As our best-moving fair solicitor.
Tell him, the daughter of the King of France,
On serious business, craving quick dispatch,
Importunes personal conference with his Grace:
Haste, signify so much; while we attend,
Like humble-visaged suitors, his high will.

Play: *Love's Labour's Lost*
Character: Princess
Genre: Comedy
Tone: Comic
Style: Verse
Act/Scene: IV i
Approx. Run Time: .40
Scene Setting: The Princess declares that she will shoot a deer on the hunt, not because she wants to but to earn praise from those with her.

See, see, my beauty will be saved by merit!
O heresy in fair, fit for these days!
A giving hand, though foul, shall have fair praise.
But come, the bow: now mercy goes to kill,
And shooting well is then accounted ill.
Thus will I save my credit in the shoot:
Not wounding, pity would not let me do't;
If wounding, then it was to show my skill,
That more for praise than purpose meant to kill.
And, out of question, so it is sometimes,
Glory grows guilty of detested crimes,
When, for fame's sake, for praise, an outward part,
We bend to that the working of the heart;
As I for praise alone now seek to spill
The poor deer's blood, that my heart means no ill.

Play: *Love's Labour's Lost*
Character: Rosaline
Genre: Comedy
Tone: Comic
Style: Verse
Act/Scene: V ii
Approx. Run Time: .30
Scene Setting: Since Biron is such a smart aleck who teases everyone, Rosaline "sentences" him to volunteer in the hospital for an entire year, telling jokes and cheering up the patients, before she will marry him.

Oft have I heard of you, my Lord Biron,
Before I saw you; and the world's large tongue
Proclaims you for a man replete with mocks,
Full of comparisons and wounding flouts,
Which you on all estates will execute
That lie within the mercy of your wit.
To weed this wormwood from your fruitful brain,
And therewithal to win me, if you please,
Without the which I am not to be won,
You shall this twelvemonth term from day to day
Visit the speechless sick, and still converse
With groaning wretches; and your task shall be,
With all the fierce endeavor of your wit
To enforce the pained impotent to smile.

Play: *Love's Labour's Lost*
Character: Rosaline
Genre: Comedy
Tone: Comic
Style: Verse
Act/Scene: V ii
Approx. Run Time: .25
Scene Setting: If Rosaline knew for a fact that she would not lose Biron for good, she would make him beg and slave to win her love.

———————>»-0-«<———————

They are worse fools to purchase mocking so.
That same Biron I'll torture ere I go:
O that I knew he were but in by the week!
How I would make him fawn, and beg, and seek,
And wait the season, and observe the times.
And spend his prodigal wits in bootless rhymes,
And shape his service wholly to my hests,
And make him proud to make me proud that jests!
So perttaunt-like would I o'ersway his state,
That he should be my fool, and I his fate.

Play: *Measure for Measure*
Character: Isabella
Genre: Comedy
Tone: Comic
Style: Verse
Act/Scene: III i
Approx. Run Time: .30
Scene Setting: Isabella is outraged that her brother wants her to sleep with Claudio to save his life.

⟫⟩◦◦⟨⟪

O you beast!
O faithless coward! O dishonest wretch!
Wilt thou be made a man out of my vice?
Is't not a kind of incest, to take life
From thine own sister's shame? What should I think?
Heaven shield my mother play'd my father fair!
For such a warped slip of wilderness
Ne'er issued from his blood. Take my defiance!
Die, perish! Might but my bending down
Reprieve thee from thy fate, it should proceed:
I'll pray a thousand prayers for thy death,
No word to save thee.
    (* *)*
O, fie, fie, fie!
Thy sin's not accidental, but a trade.
Mercy to thee would prove itself a bawd:
'Tis best that thou diest quickly.

Play: *Measure for Measure*
Character: Isabella
Genre: Comedy
Tone: Serious
Style: Verse
Act/Scene: II iv
Approx. Run Time: .40
Scene Setting: Isabella, having been improperly propositioned by Angelo to sleep with him in order to spare her brother's life, prepares to tell her brother, who she assumes will refuse such terms.

＝＝➤◆◀＝＝

To whom should I complain? Did I tell this,
Who would believe me? O perilous mouths,
That bear in them one and the self-same tongue,
Either of condemnation or approof;
Bidding the law make court'sy to their will:
Hooking both right and wrong to the appetite,
To follow as it draws! I'll to my brother:
Though he hath fallen by prompture of the blood,
Yet hath he in him such a mind of honour,
That, had he twenty heads to tender down
On twenty bloody blocks, he'ld yield them up,
Before his sister should her body stoop
To such abhorr'd pollution.
Then, Isabel, live chaste, and, brother, die:
More than our brother is our chastity.
I'll tell him yet of Angelo's request,
And fit his mind to death, for his soul's rest.
        (Exit.)

Play: *Much Ado About Nothing*
Character: Beatrice
Genre: Comedy
Tone: Comic
Style: Verse
Act/Scene: III i
Approx. Run Time: .25
Scene Setting: Beatrice, having overheard that Benedick loves her, reacts to the news.

 (Coming forward.)
What fire is in mine ears? Can this be true?
Stand I condemn'd for pride and scorn so much?
Contempt, farewell! and maiden pride, adieu!
No glory lives behind the back of such.
And, Benedick, love on; I will requite thee,
Taming my wild heart to thy loving hand:
If thou dost love, my kindness shall incite thee
To bind our loves up in a holy band;
For others say thou dost deserve, and I
Believe it better than reportingly.
 (Exit.)

Play: *Pericles, Prince of Tyre*
Character: Marina
Genre: Comedy
Tone: Serious
Style: Verse
Act/Scene: V i
Approx. Run Time: .30
Scene Setting: Marina tells a despondent stranger that she, too, has had tragedy in her life.

—————◆0◆—————

I am a maid,
My lord, that ne'er before invited eyes,
But have been gazed on like a comet: she speaks,
My lord, that, may be, hath endured a grief
Might equal yours, if both were justly weigh'd.
Though wayward fortune did malign my state,
My derivation was from ancestors
Who stood equivalent with mighty kings:
But time hath rooted out my parentage,
And to the world and awkward casualties
Bound me in servitude.
    (Aside.)
I will desist;
But there is something glows upon my cheek,
And whispers in mine ear, 'Go not till he speak.'

Play: *The Merchant of Venice*
Character: Portia
Genre: Comedy
Tone: Serious
Style: Verse
Act/Scene: IV i
Approx. Run Time: .50
Scene Setting: In disguise as a learned judge, Portia argues for Shylock to show mercy and forgive Antonio's late debt payment.

—————⇒»•◦•«⇐—————

The quality of mercy is not strain'd,
It droppeth as the gentle rain from heaven
Upon the place beneath: it is twice blest;
It blesseth him that gives and him that takes:
'Tis mightiest in the mightiest: it becomes
The throned monarch better than his crown;
His sceptre shows the force of temporal power,
The attribute to awe and majesty,
Wherein doth sit the dread and fear of kings;
But mercy is above this sceptred sway;
It is enthroned in the hearts of kings,
It is an attribute to God himself;
And earthly power doth then show likest God's
When mercy seasons justice. Therefore, Jew,
Though justice be thy plea, consider this,
That, in the course of justice, none of us
Should see salvation: we do pray for mercy;
And that same prayer doth teach us all to render
The deeds of mercy. I have spoke thus much
To mitigate the justice of thy plea;
Which if thou follow, this strict court of Venice
Must needs give sentence 'gainst the merchant there.

Play: *The Merchant of Venice*
Character: Portia
Genre: Comedy
Tone: Serious
Style: Verse
Act/Scene: III ii
Approx. Run Time: .50
Scene Setting: Portia declares her love and loyalty to Bassanio and presents him with a ring to which she attaches proof of his fidelity and love to her.

———◇◦◁———

You see me, Lord Bassanio, where I stand,
Such as I am: though for myself alone
I would not be ambitious in my wish,
To wish myself much better; yet, for you
I would be trebled twenty times myself;
A thousand times more fair, ten thousand times more rich;
That only to stand high in your account,
I might in virtue, beauties, livings, friends,
Exceed account; but the full sum of me
Is sum of something, which, to term in gross,
Is an unlesson'd girl, unschool'd, unpractised;
Happy in this, she is not yet so old
But she may learn; happier than this,
She is not bred so dull but she can learn;
Happiest of all is that her gentle spirit
Commits itself to yours to be directed,
As from her lord, her governor, her king.
Myself and what is mine to you and yours
Is now converted: but now I was the lord
Of this fair mansion, master of my servants,

Queen o'er myself; and even now, but now,
This house, these servants, and this same myself
Are yours, my lord: I give them with this ring;
Which when you part from, lose, or give away,
Let it presage the ruin of your love,
And be my vantage to exclaim on you.

Play: *The Taming of the Shrew*
Character: Katharina
Genre: Comedy
Tone: Serious
Style: Verse
Act/Scene: V ii
Approx. Run Time: 1.50
Scene Setting: Katherina, having learned the secret to controlling men is acting sweet and feigning weakness, shares this wisdom with her girlfriends — in the presence of their husbands.

———◦—◦◦◦—

Fie, fie! unknit that threatening unkind brow,
And dart not scornful glances from those eyes,
To wound thy lord, thy king, thy governor:
It blots thy beauty as frosts do bite the meads,
Confounds thy fame as whirlwinds shake fair buds,
And in no sense is meet or amiable.
A woman moved is like a fountain troubled,
Muddy, ill-seeming, thick, bereft of beauty;
And while it is so, none so dry or thirsty
Will deign to sip or touch one drop of it.
Thy husband is thy lord, thy life, thy keeper,
Thy head, thy sovereign; one that cares for thee,
And for thy maintenance commits his body
To painful labour both by sea and land,
To watch the night in storms, the day in cold,
Whilst thou liest warm at home, secure and safe;
And craves no other tribute at thy hands
But love, fair looks and true obedience;
Too little payment for so great a debt.
Such duty as the subject owes the prince
Even such a woman oweth to her husband;
And when she is froward, peevish, sullen, sour,
And not obedient to his honest will,

What is she but a foul contending rebel
And graceless traitor to her loving lord?
I am ashamed that women are so simple
To offer war where they should kneel for peace;
Or seek for rule, supremacy and sway,
When they are bound to serve, love and obey.
Why are our bodies soft and weak and smooth,
Unapt to toil and trouble in the world,
But that our soft conditions and our hearts
Should well agree with our external parts?
Come, come, you froward and unable worms!
My mind hath been as big as one of yours,
My heart as great, my reason haply more,
To bandy word for word and frown for frown;
But now I see our lances are but straws,
Our strength as weak, our weakness past compare,
That seeming to be most which we indeed least are.
Then vail your stomachs, for it is no boot,
And place your hands below your husband's foot:
In token of which duty, if he please,
My hand is ready; may it do him ease.

Play: *The Taming of the Shrew*
Character: Katharina
Genre: Comedy
Tone: Seriocomic
Style: Verse
Act/Scene: IV iii
Approx. Run Time: .35
Scene Setting: Kate wonders why her husband has locked her up with no food.

—————⟫•◦•⟪—————

The more my wrong, the more his spite appears:
What, did he marry me to famish me?
Beggars, that come unto my father's door,
Upon entreaty have a present aims;
If not, elsewhere they meet with charity:
But I, who never knew how to entreat,
Nor never needed that I should entreat,
Am starved for meat, giddy for lack of sleep,
With oaths kept waking, and with brawling fed:
And that which spites me more than all these wants,
He does it under name of perfect love;
As who should say, if I should sleep or eat,
'Twere deadly sickness or else present death.
I prithee go and get me some repast;
I care not what, so it be wholesome food.

Play: *The Tempest*
Character: Miranda
Genre: Comedy
Tone: Serious
Style: Verse
Act/Scene: I ii
Approx. Run Time: .30
Scene Setting: Miranda, having just witness the wreck of a ship at sea, asks Prospero to stop the storm he has magically caused.

———»›·o·‹«———

If by your art, my dearest father, you have
Put the wild waters in this roar, allay them.
The sky, it seems, would pour down stinking pitch,
But that the sea, mounting to the welkin's cheek,
Dashes the fire out. O, I have suffered
With those that I saw suffer! a brave vessel,
Who had, no doubt, some noble creature in her,
Dash'd all to pieces. O, the cry did knock
Against my very heart! Poor souls, they perish'd!
Had I been any god of power, I would
Have sunk the sea within the earth, or ere
It should the good ship so have swallow'd and
The fraughting souls within her.

Play: *The Winter's Tale*
Character: Hermione
Genre: Comedy
Tone: Serious
Style: Verse
Act/Scene: III ii
Approx. Run Time: 1.10
Scene Setting: Hermione declares her innocence to her husband, the King, who has accused her of infidelity and treason without any proof.

Since what I am to say must be but that
Which contradicts my accusation and
The testimony on my part no other
But what comes from myself, it shall scarce boot me
To say 'not guilty': mine integrity
Being counted falsehood, shall, as I express it,
Be so received. But thus, if powers divine
Behold our human actions, as they do,
I doubt not then but innocence shall make
False accusation blush and tyranny
Tremble at patience. You, my lord, best know,
Who least will seem to do so, my past life
Hath been as continent, as chaste, as true,
As I am now unhappy; which is more
Than history can pattern, though devised
And play'd to take spectators. For behold me
A fellow of the royal bed, which owe
A moiety of the throne, a great king's daughter,
The mother to a hopeful prince, here standing
To prate and talk for life and honour 'fore
Who please to come and hear. For life, I prize it
As I weigh grief, which I would spare: for honour,
'Tis a derivative from me to mine,

And only that I stand for. I appeal
To your own conscience, sir, before Polixenes
Came to your court, how I was in your grace,
How merited to be so; since he came,
With what encounter so uncurrent I
Have strain'd, to appear thus: if one jot beyond
The bound of honour, or in act or will
That way inclining, harden'd be the hearts
Of all that hear me, and my near'st of kin
Cry fie upon my grave!

Play: *The Winter's Tale*
Character: Hermione
Genre: Comedy
Tone: Serious
Style: Verse
Act/Scene: III ii
Approx. Run Time: 1.00
Scene Setting: When her husband threatens her with execution, Hermione protests that she no longer has any reason to live except to defend her honor.

———◆———

Sir, spare your threats:
The bug which you would fright me with I seek.
To me can life be no commodity:
The crown and comfort of my life, your favour,
I do give lost; for I do feel it gone,
But know not how it went. My second joy
And first-fruits of my body, from his presence
I am barr'd, like one infectious. My third comfort,
Starr'd most unluckily, is from my breast,
The innocent milk in its most innocent mouth,
Haled out to murder: myself on every post
Proclaimed a strumpet: with immodest hatred
The child-bed privilege denied, which 'longs
To women of all fashion; lastly, hurried
Here to this place, i' the open air, before
I have got strength of limit. Now, my liege,
Tell me what blessings I have here alive,
That I should fear to die? Therefore proceed.
But yet hear this; mistake me not; no life,
I prize it not a straw, but for mine honour,
Which I would free, if I shall be condemn'd
Upon surmises, all proofs sleeping else
But what your jealousies awake, I tell you
'Tis rigor and not law. Your honours all,
I do refer me to the oracle;
Apollo be my judge!

Play: *Troilus and Cressida*
Character: Cressida
Genre: Comedy
Tone: Seriocomic
Style: Verse
Act/Scene: III ii
Approx. Run Time: .40
Scene Setting: Cressida declares her love coyly and using the utmost feminine wiles.

Hard to seem won: but I was won, my lord,
With the first glance that ever — pardon me;
If I confess much, you will play the tyrant.
I love you now; but not, till now, so much
But I might master it: in faith, I lie;
My thoughts were like unbridled children, grown
Too headstrong for their mother. See, we fools!
Why have I blabb'd? who shall be true to us,
When we are so unsecret to ourselves?
But, though I loved you well, I woo'd you not;
And yet, good faith, I wish'd myself a man,
Or that we women had men's privilege
Of speaking first. Sweet, bid me hold my tongue,
For in this rapture I shall surely speak
The thing I shall repent. See, see, your silence,
Cunning in dumbness, from my weakness draws
My very soul of counsel! Stop my mouth.

Play: *Twelfth Night*
Character: Olivia
Genre: Comedy
Tone: Seriocomic
Style: Verse
Act/Scene: III i
Approx. Run Time: .30
Scene Setting: Olivia is completely smitten with the Duke's serving man, who is actually Viola disguised as a boy.

O, what a deal of scorn looks beautiful
In the contempt and anger of his lip!
A murderous guilt shows not itself more soon
Than love that would seem hid: love's night is noon.
Cesario, by the roses of the spring,
By maidhood, honour, truth and every thing,
I love thee so, that, maugre all thy pride,
Nor wit nor reason can my passion hide.
Do not extort thy reasons from this clause,
For that I woo, thou therefore hast no cause;
But rather reason thus with reason fetter,
Love sought is good, but given unsought better.

Play: *Twelfth Night*
Character: Olivia
Genre: Comedy
Tone: Seriocomic
Style: Verse
Act/Scene: I v
Approx. Run Time: .40
Scene Setting: Completely charmed by the Duke's mysterious new serving man, Olivia devises a way to get the youth to return to her.

'What is your parentage?'
'Above my fortunes, yet my state is well:
I am a gentleman.' I'll be sworn thou art;
Thy tongue, thy face, thy limbs, actions and spirit,
Do give thee five-fold blazon: not too fast: soft, soft!
Unless the master were the man. How now!
Even so quickly may one catch the plague?
Methinks I feel this youth's perfections
With an invisible and subtle stealth
To creep in at mine eyes. Well, let it be.
What ho, Malvolio!
       (* *)*
Run after that same peevish messenger,
The county's man: he left this ring behind him,
Would I or not: tell him I'll none of it.
Desire him not to flatter with his lord,
Nor hold him up with hopes; I am not for him:
If that the youth will come this way to-morrow,
I'll give him reasons for't: hie thee, Malvolio.

Play: *Twelfth Night*
Character: Viola
Genre: Comedy
Tone: Comic
Style: Verse
Act/Scene: II ii
Approx. Run Time: 1.00
Scene Setting: Viola is given a ring by Olivia's steward and realizes Olivia must have fallen in love with her believing that she is a man.

>➤◦◄

I left no ring with her: what means this lady?
Fortune forbid my outside have not charm'd her!
She made good view of me; indeed, so much,
That sure methought her eyes had lost her tongue,
For she did speak in starts distractedly.
She loves me, sure; the cunning of her passion
Invites me in this churlish messenger.
None of my lord's ring! why, he sent her none.
I am the man: if it be so, as 'tis,
Poor lady, she were better love a dream.
Disguise, I see, thou art a wickedness,
Wherein the pregnant enemy does much.
How easy is it for the proper-false
In women's waxen hearts to set their forms!
Alas, our frailty is the cause, not we!
For such as we are made of, such we be.
How will this fadge? my master loves her dearly;
And I, poor monster, fond as much on him;
And she, mistaken, seems to dote on me.
What will become of this? As I am man,
My state is desperate for my master's love;
As I am woman, — now alas the day! —
What thriftless sighs shall poor Olivia breathe!
O time! thou must untangle this, not I;
It is too hard a knot for me to untie!
　　(Exit.)

Play: *Two Gentlemen of Verona*
Character: Julia
Genre: Comedy
Tone: Serious
Style: Verse
Act/Scene: IV iv
Approx. Run Time: .40
Scene Setting: Julia, in disguise, agrees to woo another woman on behalf of the man she loves.

———————

How many women would do such a message?
Alas, poor Proteus! thou hast entertain'd
A fox to be the shepherd of thy lambs.
Alas, poor fool! why do I pity him
That with his very heart despiseth me?
Because he loves her, he despiseth me;
Because I love him, I must pity him.
This ring I gave him when he parted from me,
To bind him to remember my good will;
And now am I, unhappy messenger,
To plead for that which I would not obtain,
To carry that which I would have refused,
To praise his faith which I would have dispraised.
I am my master's true-confirmed love;
But cannot be true servant to my master,
Unless I prove false traitor to myself.
Yet will I woo for him, but yet so coldly,
As, heaven it knows, I would not have him speed.

Play: *Two Gentlemen of Verona*
Character: Julia
Genre: Comedy
Tone: Seriocomic
Style: Verse
Act/Scene: I ii
Approx. Run Time: 1.00
Scene Setting: Julia berates herself for tearing up a letter from the man she loves.

—————⇒►-◊-◄⇐—————

Nay, would I were so anger'd with the same!
O hateful hands, to tear such loving words!
Injurious wasps, to feed on such sweet honey
And kill the bees that yield it, with your stings!
I'll kiss each several paper for amends.
Look, here is writ 'kind Julia.' Unkind Julia!
As in revenge of thy ingratitude,
I throw thy name against the bruising stones,
Trampling contemptuously on thy disdain.
And here is writ 'love-wounded Proteus.'
Poor wounded name! my bosom, as a bed,
Shall lodge thee, till thy wound be thoroughly heal'd;
And thus I search it with a sovereign kiss.
But twice or thrice was 'Proteus' written down.
Be calm, good wind, blow not a word away
Till I have found each letter in the letter,
Except mine own name: that some whirlwind bear
Unto a ragged, fearful-hanging rock
And throw it thence into the raging sea!
Lo, here in one line is his name twice writ,
'Poor forlorn Proteus, passionate Proteus,
To the sweet Julia': — that I'll tear away. —
And yet I will not, sith so prettily
He couples it to his complaining names.
Thus will I fold them one upon another:
Now kiss, embrace, contend, do what you will.

Play: *Henry IV Part I*
Character: Lady Percy
Genre: History
Tone: Serious
Style: Verse
Act/Scene: II iii
Approx. Run Time: 1.05
Scene Setting: Lady Percy fears that her young husband is more attracted to the details of war than to her; she fears he is not telling her his plans.

O, my good lord, why are you thus alone?
For what offence have I this fortnight been
A banish'd woman from my Harry's bed?
Tell me, sweet lord, what is't that takes from thee,
Thy stomach, pleasure, and thy golden sleep?
Why dost thou bend thine eyes upon the earth,
And start so often when thou sit'st alone?
Why hast thou lost the fresh blood in thy cheeks;
And given my treasures and my rights of thee
To thick-eyed musing and cursed melancholy?
In thy faint slumbers I by thee have watch'd,
And heard thee murmur tales of iron wars;
Speak terms of manage to thy bounding steed;
Cry 'Courage! to the field!' And thou hast talk'd
Of sallies and retires, of trenches, tents,
Of palisadoes, frontiers, parapets,
Of basilisks, of cannon, culverin,
Of prisoners' ransom and of soldiers slain,
And all the currents of a heady fight.
Thy spirit within thee hath been so at war
And thus hath so bestirr'd thee in thy sleep,
That beads of sweat have stood upon thy brow
Like bubbles in a late-disturbed stream;

And in thy face strange motions have appear'd,
Such as we see when men restrain their breath
On some great sudden hest. O, what portents are these?
Some heavy business hath my lord in hand,
And I must know it, else he loves me not.

Play: *Henry IV Part II*
Character: Lady Percy
Genre: History
Tone: Serious
Style: Verse
Act/Scene: II iii
Approx. Run Time: 1.25
Scene Setting: Lady Percy lambasts Northumberland for committing forces to the Archbishop when he left his own son (Lady Percy's husband) and his army to die in a previous battle.

O yet, for God's sake, go not to these wars!
The time was, father, that you broke your word,
When you were more endeared to it than now;
When your own Percy, when my heart's dear Harry,
Threw many a northward look to see his father
Bring up his powers; but he did long in vain.
Who then persuaded you to stay at home?
There were two honours lost, yours and your son's.
For yours, the God of heaven brighten it!
For his, it stuck upon him as the sun
In the grey vault of heaven, and by his light
Did all the chivalry of England move
To do brave acts: he was indeed the glass
Wherein the noble youth did dress themselves:
He had no legs that practised not his gait;
And speaking thick, which nature made his blemish,
Became the accents of the valiant;
For those that could speak low and tardily
Would turn their own perfection to abuse,
To seem like him: so that in speech, in gait,
In diet, in affections of delight,
In military rules, humours of blood,
He was the mark and glass, copy and book,

That fashion'd others. And him, O wondrous him!
O miracle of men! him did you leave,
Second to none, unseconded by you,
To look upon the hideous god of war
In disadvantage; to abide a field
Where nothing but the sound of Hotspur's name
Did seem defensible: so you left him.
Never, O never, do his ghost the wrong
To hold your honour more precise and nice
With others than with him! let them alone:
The marshal and the archbishop are strong:
Had my sweet Harry had but half their numbers,
To-day might I, hanging on Hotspur's neck,
Have talk'd of Monmouth's grave.

Play: *Henry VI Part I*
Character: Joan La Pucelle
Genre: History
Tone: Serious
Style: Verse
Act/Scene: V iv
Approx. Run Time: .40
Scene Setting: The captured French heroine Joan, on trial for treason and witchcraft by the English, defends herself from execution.

—————◆◆◆◆◆—————

First, let me tell you whom you have condemn'd:
Not me begotten of a shepherd swain,
But issued from the progeny of kings;
Virtuous and holy; chosen from above,
By inspiration of celestial grace,
To work exceeding miracles on earth.
I never had to do with wicked spirits:
But you, that are polluted with your lusts,
Stain'd with the guiltless blood of innocents,
Corrupt and tainted with a thousand vices,
Because you want the grace that others have,
You judge it straight a thing impossible
To compass wonders but by help of devils.
No, misconceived! Joan of Arc hath been
A virgin from her tender infancy,
Chaste and immaculate in very thought;
Whose maiden blood, thus rigorously effused,
Will cry for vengeance at the gates of heaven.

Play: *Henry VI Part I*
Character: Joan La Pucelle
Genre: History
Tone: Serious
Style: Verse
Act/Scene: III iii
Approx. Run Time: .35
Scene Setting: Joan expresses her patriotic feeling toward her motherland.

Look on thy country, look on fertile France,
And see the cities and the towns defaced
By wasting ruin of the cruel foe.
As looks the mother on her lowly babe
When death doth close his tender dying eyes,
See, see the pining malady of France;
Behold the wounds, the most unnatural wounds,
Which thou thyself hast given her woful breast.
O, turn thy edged sword another way;
Strike those that hurt, and hurt not those that help.
One drop of blood drawn from thy country's bosom
Should grieve thee more than streams of foreign gore:
Return thee therefore with a flood of tears,
And wash away thy country's stained spots.

Play: *Richard III*
Character: Anne
Genre: History
Tone: Serious
Style: Verse
Act/Scene: IV i
Approx. Run Time: .50
Scene Setting: As the new wife of Richard, Anne realizes she has become the subject of her own curse, since she wished ill on the next woman to marry him.

⊷⊶⊷

No! why? When he that is my husband now
Came to me, as I follow'd Henry's corse,
When scarce the blood was well wash'd from his hands
Which issued from my other angel husband
And that dead saint which then I weeping follow'd;
O, when, I say, I look'd on Richard's face,
This was my wish: 'Be thou,' quoth I, 'accursed,
For making me, so young, so old a widow!
And, when thou wed'st, let sorrow haunt thy bed;
And be thy wife — if any be so mad —
As miserable by the life of thee
As thou hast made me by my dear lord's death!'
Lo, ere I can repeat this curse again,
Even in so short a space, my woman's heart
Grossly grew captive to his honey words,
And proved the subject of my own soul's curse,
Which ever since hath kept my eyes from rest;
For never yet one hour in his bed
Have I enjoy'd the golden dew of sleep,
But have been waked by his timorous dreams.
Besides, he hates me for my father Warwick;
And will, no doubt, shortly be rid of me.

Play: *Richard III*
Character: Anne
Genre: History
Tone: Serious
Style: Verse
Act/Scene: I ii
Approx. Run Time: 1.15
Scene Setting: Anne stops the funeral procession of the murdered King Henry to grieve over his body and curse Richard III, the man who murdered both the king and her own husband.

———➤•◄———

Set down, set down your honourable load —
If honour may be shrouded in a hearse —
Whilst I awhile obsequiously lament
The untimely fall of virtuous Lancaster.
Poor key-cold figure of a holy king!
Pale ashes of the house of Lancaster!
Thou bloodless remnant of that royal blood!
Be it lawful that I invocate thy ghost,
To hear the lamentations of poor Anne,
Wife to thy Edward, to thy slaughter'd son,
Stabb'd by the selfsame hand that made these wounds!
Lo, in these windows that let forth thy life,
I pour the helpless balm of my poor eyes.
Cursed be the hand that made these fatal holes!
Cursed be the heart that had the heart to do it!
Cursed the blood that let this blood from hence!
More direful hap betide that hated wretch,
That makes us wretched by the death of thee,
Than I can wish to adders, spiders, toads,
Or any creeping venom'd thing that lives!
If ever he have child, abortive be it,
Prodigious, and untimely brought to light,
Whose ugly and unnatural aspect

May fright the hopeful mother at the view;
And that be heir to his unhappiness!
If ever he have wife, let her he made
A miserable by the death of him
As I am made by my poor lord and thee!
Come, now towards Chertsey with your holy load,
Taken from Paul's to be interred there;
And still, as you are weary of the weight,
Rest you, whiles I lament King Henry's corse.

Play: *Hamlet*
Character: Ophelia
Genre: Tragedy
Tone: Serious
Style: Verse
Act/Scene: II i
Approx. Run Time: .50
Scene Setting: Ophelia describes for her father how strangely Hamlet has behaved with her.

———⇒▷◦◁⇐———

O, my lord, my lord, I have been so affrighted!
    (* *)*
My lord, as I was sewing in my closet,
Lord Hamlet, with his doublet all unbraced,
No hat upon his head, his stockings foul'd,
Ungarter'd, and down-gyved to his ancle;
Pale as his shirt, his knees knocking each other,
And with a look so piteous in purport
As if he had been loosed out of hell
To speak of horrors, he comes before me.
    (* *)*
He took me by the wrist and held me hard;
Then goes he to the length of all his arm,
And with his other hand thus o'er his brow,
He falls to such perusal of my face
As he would draw it. Long stay'd he so;
At last, a little shaking of mine arm
And thrice his head thus waving up and down,
He raised a sigh so piteous and profound
As it did seem to shatter all his bulk
And end his being: that done, he lets me go:
And, with his head over his shoulder turn'd,
He seem'd to find his way without his eyes;
For out o' doors he went without their helps,
And, to the last, bended their light on me.

Play: *Hamlet*
Character: Ophelia
Genre: Tragedy
Tone: Serious
Style: Verse
Act/Scene: III i
Approx. Run Time: .30
Scene Setting: Ophelia is shocked by Hamlet's strange new behavior.

O, what a noble mind is here o'erthrown!
The courtier's, soldier's, scholar's, eye, tongue, sword:
The expectancy and rose of the fair state,
The glass of fashion and the mould of form,
The observed of all observers, quite, quite down!
And I, of ladies most deject and wretched,
That suck'd the honey of his music vows,
Now see that noble and most sovereign reason,
Like sweet bells jangled, out of tune and harsh;
That unmatch'd form and feature of blown youth
Blasted with ecstasy: O, woe is me,
To have seen what I have seen, see what I see!

Play: *Julius Caesar*
Character: Portia
Genre: Tragedy
Tone: Serious
Style: Verse
Act/Scene: II i
Approx. Run Time: .40
Scene Setting: Portia demands that her husband share with her the secrets she knows are eating at him.

Is Brutus sick, and is it physical
To walk unbraced and suck up the humours
Of the dank morning? What, is Brutus sick,
And will he steal out of his wholesome bed,
To dare the vile contagion of the night,
And tempt the rheumy and unpurged air
To add unto his sickness? No, my Brutus;
You have some sick offence within your mind,
Which, by the right and virtue of my place
I ought to know of: and, upon my knees,
I charm you, by my once commended beauty,
By all your vows of love and that great vow
Which did incorporate and make us one,
That you unfold to me, yourself, your half,
Why you are heavy, and what men to-night
Have had to resort to you; for here have been
Some six or seven, who did hide their faces
Even from darkness.

Play: *King Lear*
Character: Cordelia
Genre: Tragedy
Tone: Serious
Style: Verse
Act/Scene: I i
Approx. Run Time: .30
Scene Setting: After hearing her two sisters falsely flatter their father to ensure themselves large dowries, Cordelia professes her love for him simply and truthfully.

━━━➤◦◄━━━

Unhappy that I am, I cannot heave
My heart into my mouth: I love your majesty
According to my bond; nor more nor less.
  (* *)*
Good my lord,
You have begot me, bred me, loved me: I
Return those duties back as are right fit,
Obey you, love you, and most honour you.
Why have my sisters husbands, if they say
They love you all? Haply, when I shall wed,
That lord whose hand must take my plight shall carry
Half my love with him, half my care and duty:
Sure, I shall never marry like my sisters,
To love my father all.

Play: *Othello*
Character: Desdemona
Genre: Tragedy
Tone: Serious
Style: Verse
Act/Scene: I iii
Approx. Run Time: .20
Scene Setting: Desdemona explains to her father that since she has married Othello, she now gives her husband her primary allegiance.

———➤◦◄———

My noble father,
I do perceive here a divided duty:
To you I am bound for life and education;
My life and education both do learn me
How to respect you; you are the lord of duty,
I am hitherto your daughter: but here's my husband,
And so much duty as my mother show'd
To you, preferring you before her father,
So much I challenge that I may profess
Due to the Moor my lord.

Play: *Othello*
Character: Desdemona
Genre: Tragedy
Tone: Serious
Style: Verse
Act/Scene: IV ii
Approx. Run Time: .35
Scene Setting: Desdemona asks Iago for his advice on how to win back favor with her husband after he has denounced her as a "whore." Ironically, it is Iago who has turned her husband jealously against her.

———◦———

O good Iago,
What shall I do to win my lord again?
Good friend, go to him; for, by this light of heaven,
I know not how I lost him. Here I kneel:
If e'er my will did trespass 'gainst his love,
Either in discourse of thought or actual deed,
Or that mine eyes, mine ears, or any sense,
Delighted them in any other form,
Or that I do not yet, and ever did,
And ever will, though he do shake me off
To beggarly divorcement, love him dearly,
Comfort forswear me! Unkindness may do much;
And his unkindness may defeat my life,
But never taint my love. I cannot say 'whore':
It does abhor me now I speak the word;
To do the act that might the addition earn
Not the world's mass of vanity could make me.

Play: *Othello*
Character: Desdemona
Genre: Tragedy
Tone: Serious
Style: Verse
Act/Scene: I iii
Approx. Run Time: .30
Scene Setting: Desdemona begs to be allowed to accompany her husband to his newly assigned post.

⇒➤•◀⇐

That I did love the Moor to live with him,
My downright violence and storm of fortunes
May trumpet to the world: my heart's subdued
Even to the very quality of my lord:
I saw Othello's visage in his mind,
And to his honour and his valiant parts
Did I my soul and fortunes consecrate.
So that, dear lords, if I be left behind,
A moth of peace, and he go to the war,
The rites for which I love him are bereft me,
And I a heavy interim shall support
By his dear absence. Let me go with him.

Play: *Romeo and Juliet*
Character: Juliet
Genre: Tragedy
Tone: Serious
Style: Verse
Act/Scene: III ii
Approx. Run Time: 1.15
Scene Setting: Juliet has secretly married Romeo and awaits his arrival on their first night together.

———➤◦◄———

Gallop apace, you fiery-footed steeds,
Towards Phoebus' lodging: such a wagoner
As Phaethon would whip you to the west,
And bring in cloudy night immediately.
Spread thy close curtain, love-performing night,
That runaways' eyes may wink, and Romeo
Leap to these arms, untalk'd of and unseen.
Lovers can see to do their amorous rites
By their own beauties; or, if love be blind,
It best agrees with night. Come, civil night,
Thou sober-suited matron, all in black,
And learn me how to lose a winning match,
Play'd for a pair of stainless maidenhoods:
Hood my unmann'd blood bating in my cheeks
With thy black mantle, till strange love grown bold
Think true love acted simple modesty.
Come, night; come, Romeo, come, thou day in night;
For thou wilt lie upon the wings of night
Whiter than new snow on a raven's back.
Come, gentle night, come, loving, black-brow'd night,
Give me my Romeo; and, when he shall die,
Take him and cut him out in little stars,
And he will make the face of heaven so fine,
That all the world will be in love with night,

And pay no worship to the garish sun.
O, I have bought the mansion of a love,
But not possess'd it, and, though I am sold,
Not yet enjoy'd; so tedious is this day
As is the night before some festival
To an impatient child that hath new robes
And may not wear them. O, here comes my nurse,
And she brings news, and every tongue that speaks
But Romeo's name speaks heavenly eloquence.

Play: *Romeo and Juliet*
Character: Juliet
Genre: Tragedy
Tone: Comic
Style: Verse
Act/Scene: II v
Approx. Run Time: .40
Scene Setting: Juliet has sent her nurse to Romeo to arrange for their secret marriage and waits for the nurse to return.

————⇒●◅————

The clock struck nine when I did send the nurse;
In half an hour she promised to return.
Perchance she cannot meet him: that's not so.
O, she is lame! love's heralds should be thoughts,
Which ten times faster glide than the sun's beams,
Driving back shadows over louring hills:
Therefore do nimble-pinion'd doves draw love,
And therefore hath the wind-swift Cupid wings.
Now is the sun upon the highmost hill
Of this day's journey, and from nine till twelve
Is three long hours; yet she is not come.
Had she affections and warm youthful blood,
She would be as swift in motion as a ball;
My words would bandy her to my sweet love,
And his to me:
But old folks, many feign as they were dead;
Unwieldy, slow, heavy and pale as lead.
    (Enter Nurse.)
O God, she comes!

Play: *Romeo and Juliet*
Character: Juliet
Genre: Tragedy
Tone: Seriocomic
Style: Verse
Act/Scene: II ii
Approx. Run Time: 1.00
Scene Setting: Juliet has wildly declared her love and now wonders if she should have been more coy.

Thou know'st the mask of night is on my face,
Else would a maiden blush bepaint my cheek
For that which thou hast heard me speak to-night
Fain would I dwell on form, fain, fain deny
What I have spoke: but farewell compliment!
Dost thou love me? I know thou wilt say 'Ay,'
And I will take thy word: yet if thou swear'st,
Thou mayst prove false: at lovers' perjuries,
They say, Jove laughs. O gentle Romeo,
If thou dost love, pronounce it faithfully:
Or if thou think'st I am too quickly won,
I'll frown and be perverse and say thee nay,
So thou wilt woo; but else, not for the world.
In truth, fair Montague, I am too fond;
And therefore thou mayst think my 'havior light:
But trust me, gentleman, I'll prove more true
Than those that have more cunning to be strange.
I should have been more strange, I must confess,
But that thou overheard'st, ere I was ware,
My true love's passion: therefore pardon me,
And not impute this yielding to light love,
Which the dark night hath so discovered.

MALE
MONOLOGUES

Play: *A Midsummer Night's Dream*
Character: Demetrius
Genre: Comedy
Tone: Seriocomic
Style: Verse
Act/Scene: IV i
Approx. Run Time: .35
Scene Setting: Demetrius explains why he followed the eloping Lysander and Hermia and how his heart has turned back to Helena during their adventures.

My lord, fair Helen told me of their stealth,
Of this their purpose hither to this wood;
And I in fury hither follow'd them,
Fair Helena in fancy following me.
But, my good lord, I wot not by what power, —
But by some power it is, — my love to Hermia,
Melted as the snow, seems to me now
As the remembrance of an idle gaud,
Which in my childhood I did dote upon;
And all the faith, the virtue of my heart,
The object and the pleasure of mine eye,
Is only Helena. To her, my lord,
Was I betroth'd ere I saw Hermia:
But, like in sickness, did I loathe this food;
But, as in health, come to my natural taste,
Now I do wish it, love it, long for it,
And will for evermore be true to it.

Play: *A Midsummer Night's Dream*
Character: Lysander
Genre: Comedy
Tone: Seriocomic
Style: Verse
Act/Scene: I i
Approx. Run Time: .30
Scene Setting: Lysander makes a stand for his romance with Hermia, though her father wants her to marry Demetrius.

➤●◄

You have her father's love, Demetrius;
Let me have Hermia's: do you marry him.
   (* *)*
I am, my lord, as well derived as he,
As well possess'd; my love is more than his;
My fortunes every way as fairly rank'd,
If not with vantage, as Demetrius';
And, which is more than all these boasts can be,
I am beloved of beauteous Hermia:
Why should not I then prosecute my right?
Demetrius, I'll avouch it to his head,
Made love to Nedar's daughter, Helena,
And won her soul; and she, sweet lady, dotes,
Devoutly dotes, dotes in idolatry,
Upon this spotted and inconstant man.

Play: *A Midsummer Night's Dream*

Character: Quince

Genre: Comedy

Tone: Comic

Style: Verse

Act/Scene: V i

Approx. Run Time: 1.30

Scene Setting: Amateur actor Quince delivers the Prologue of a play that his group performs for the Duke.

(Enter Qunice for the Prologue.)
If we offend, it is with our good will.
That you should think, we come not to offend,
But with good will. To show our simple skill,
That is the true beginning of our end.
Consider, then, we come but in despite.
We do not come, as minding to content you,
Our true intent is. All for your delight,
We are not here. That you should here repent you,
The actors are at hand; and by their show,
You shall know all, that you are like to know.
   (* * *)
Gentles, perchance you wonder at this show;
But wonder on, till truth make all things plain.
This man is Pyramus, if you would know;
This beauteous lady Thisbe is certain.
This man, with lime and rough-cast, doth present
Wall, that vile Wall which did these lovers sunder;
And through Wall's chink, poor souls, they are content
To whisper. At the which let no man wonder.
This man, with lanthorn, dog, and bush of thorn,
Presenteth Moonshine; for, if you will know,
By moonshine did these lovers think no scorn
To meet at Ninus' tomb, there, there to woo.

This grisly beast, which Lion hight by name,
The trusty Thisbe, coming first by night,
Did scare away, or rather did affright;
And, as she fled, her mantle she did fall,
Which Lion vile with bloody mouth did stain.
Anon comes Pyramus, sweet youth and tall,
And finds his trusty Thisbe's mantle slain:
Whereat, with blade, with bloody blameful blade,
He bravely broach'd his boiling bloody breast;
And Thisbe, tarrying in mulberry shade,
His dagger drew, and died. For all the rest,
Let Lion, Moonshine, Wall, and lovers twain
At large discourse, while here they do remain.

Play: *All's Well That Ends Well*

Character: Bertram

Genre: Comedy

Tone: Seriocomic

Style: Verse

Act/Scene: IV ii

Approx. Run Time: .20

Scene Setting: Bertram, trying to seduce Diana, tells her not to be so cold.

———→•◦◦•←———

Titled goddess;
And worth it, with addition! But, fair soul,
In your fine frame hath love no quality?
If quick fire of youth light not your mind,
You are no maiden, but a monument:
When you are dead, you should be such a one
As you are now, for you are cold and stern;
And now you should be as your mother was
When your sweet self was got.

Play: *As You Like It*
Character: Jaques
Genre: Comedy
Tone: Seriocomic
Style: Verse
Act/Scene: II vii
Approx. Run Time: 1.10
Scene Setting: A philosophizing cynic, the dour yet sentimental Jaques explains the seven phases of a man's life.

—————

All the world's a stage,
And all the men and women merely players:
They have their exits and their entrances;
And one man in his time plays many parts,
His acts being seven ages. At first the infant,
Mewling and puking in the nurse's arms.
And then the whining school-boy, with his satchel
And shining morning face, creeping like snail
Unwillingly to school. And then the lover,
Sighing like furnace, with a woeful ballad
Made to his mistress' eyebrow. Then a soldier,
Full of strange oaths, and bearded like the pard,
Jealous in honour, sudden and quick in quarrel,
Seeking the bubble reputation
Even in the cannon's mouth. And then the justice,
In fair round belly with good capon lined,
With eyes severe and beard of formal cut,
Full of wise saws and modern instances;
And so he plays his part. The sixth age shifts
Into the lean and slipper'd pantaloon,
With spectacles on nose and pouch on side,
His youthful hose, well saved, a world too wide

For his shrunk shank; and his big manly voice,
Turning again toward childish treble, pipes
And whistles in his sound. Last scene of all,
That ends this strange eventful history,
Is second childishness and mere oblivion,
Sans teeth, sans eyes, sans taste, sans everything.

Play: *As You Like It*
Character: Oliver
Genre: Comedy
Tone: Seriocomic
Style: Prose
Act/Scene: I i
Approx. Run Time: .55
Scene Setting: Warned that his brother, Orlando, is determined to challenge Charles, the local wrestling star (who does not want to fight Orlando for fear of hurting him), Oliver sets his brother up for a beating by insisting that Orlando is dangerous and sneaky and will stop at nothing to win.

————⟫•◦•⟪————

Charles, I thank thee for thy love to me, which thou shalt find I will most kindly requite. I had myself notice of my brother's purpose herein, and have by underhand means laboured to dissuade him from it, but he is resolute. I'll tell thee, Charles: — it is the stubbornest young fellow of France, full of ambition, an envious emulator of every man's good parts, a secret and villanous contriver against me his natural brother: therefore use thy discretion; I had as lief thou didst break his neck as his finger. And thou wert best look to't; for if thou dost him any slight disgrace, or if he do not mightily grace himself on thee, he will practise against thee by poison, entrap thee by some treacherous device, and never leave thee till he hath ta'en thy life by some indirect means or other; for, I assure thee, and almost with tears I speak it, there is not one so young and so villanous this day living. I speak but brotherly of him; but should I anatomize him to thee as he is, I must blush and weep, and thou must look pale and wonder.

Play: *As You Like It*
Character: Oliver
Genre: Comedy
Tone: Seriocomic
Style: Verse
Act/Scene: IV iii
Approx. Run Time: .50
Scene Setting: Oliver explains how his brother Orlando has just saved his life.

———◦———

When last the young Orlando parted from you
He left a promise to return again
Within an hour, and pacing through the forest,
Chewing the food of sweet and bitter fancy,
Lo, what befel! he threw his eye aside,
And mark what object did present itself:
Under an oak, whose boughs were moss'd with age
And high top bald with dry antiquity,
A wretched ragged man, o'ergrown with hair,
Lay sleeping on his back: about his neck
A green and gilded snake had wreathed itself,
Who with her head nimble in threats approach'd
The opening of his mouth; but suddenly,
Seeing Orlando, it unlink'd itself,
And with indented glides did slip away
Into a bush: under which bush's shade
A lioness, with udders all drawn dry,
Lay couching, head on ground, with catlike watch,
When that the sleeping man should stir; for 'tis
The royal disposition of that beast
To prey on nothing that doth seem as dead:
This seen, Orlando did approach the man
And found it was his brother, his elder brother.

Play: *As You Like It*
Character: Orlando
Genre: Comedy
Tone: Seriocomic
Style: Prose
Act/Scene: I i
Approx. Run Time: 1.00
Scene Setting: Orlando describes the rough treatment his guardian and brother, Oliver, gives him.

————⟫-◦-⟨————

As I remember, Adam, it was upon this fashion: bequeathed me by will but poor a thousand crowns, and, as thou sayest, charged my brother, on his blessing, to breed me well: and there begins my sadness. My brother Jaques he keeps at school, and report speaks goldenly of his profit: for my part, he keeps me rustically at home, or, to speak more properly, stays me here at home unkept; for call you that keeping for a gentleman of my birth, that differs not from the stalling of an ox? His horses are bred better; for, besides that they are fair with their feeding, they are taught their manage, and to that end riders dearly hired: but I, his brother, gain nothing under him but growth; for the which his animals on his dunghills are as much bound to him as I. Besides this nothing that he so plentifully gives me, the something that nature gave me his countenance seems to take from me: he lets me feed with his hinds, bars me the place of a brother, and, as much as in him lies, mines my gentility with my education. This is it, Adam, that grieves me; and the spirit of my father, which I think is within me, begins to mutiny against this servitude: I will no longer endure it, though yet I know no wise remedy how to avoid it.

Play: *As You Like It*
Character: Orlando
Genre: Comedy
Tone: Seriocomic
Style: Prose
Act/Scene: I ii
Approx. Run Time: .30
Scene Setting: Orlando responds that he has nothing to lose by challenging the wrestler Charles to a fight, though Rosalind and Celia beg him not to.

I beseech you, punish me not with your hard thoughts; wherein I confess me much guilty, to deny so fair and excellent ladies any thing. But let your fair eyes and gentle wishes go with me to my trial: wherein if I be foiled, there is but one shamed that was never gracious; if killed, but one dead that was willing to be so: I shall do my friends no wrong, for I have none to lament me, the world no injury, for in it I have nothing: only in the world I fill up a place, which may be better supplied when I have made it empty.

Play: *As You Like It*
Character: Orlando
Genre: Comedy
Tone: Serious
Style: Verse
Act/Scene: II vi
Approx. Run Time: .40
Scene Setting: Orlando, lost in the forest with Adam, begs him to hang on while he finds food and shelter.

Why, how now, Adam! no greater heart in thee?
Live a little; comfort a little; cheer thyself a little.
If this uncouth forest yield any thing savage, I
will either be food for it or bring it for food to
thee. Thy conceit is nearer death than thy powers.
For my sake be comfortable; hold death awhile at
the arm's end: I will here be with thee presently;
and if I bring thee not something to eat, I will
give thee leave to die: but if thou diest before I
come, thou art a mocker of my labour. Well said!
thou lookest cheerly, and I'll be with thee quickly.
Yet thou liest in the bleak air: come, I will bear
thee to some shelter; and thou shalt not die for
lack of a dinner, if there live any thing in this
desert. Cheerly, good Adam!

Play: *Cymbeline*
Character: Posthumus
Genre: Comedy
Tone: Serious
Style: Verse
Act/Scene: V iv
Approx. Run Time: 1.15
Scene Setting: Waking from a dream in which the ghosts of his parents and family ask the god Jupiter to take pity on him, Posthumus finds a book with a prophetic message he cannot decipher.

(Waking.)
Sleep, thou hast been a grandsire, and begot
A father to me; and thou hast created
A mother and two brothers: but, O scorn!
Gone! they went hence so soon as they were born:
And so I am awake. Poor wretches that depend
On greatness' favour dream as I have done;
Wake and find nothing. But, alas, I swerve:
Many dream not to find, neither deserve,
And yet are steep'd in favours; so am I,
That have this golden chance, and know not why.
What fairies haunt this ground? A book? O rare one!
Be not, as is our fangled world, a garment
Nobler than that it covers: let thy effects
So follow, to be most unlike our courtiers,
As good as promise.
(Reads.)
"When as a lion's whelp shall, to himself unknown, without seeking find, and shall be embraced by a piece to tender air; and when from a stately cedar shall be lopped branches, which, being dead many years, shall after revive, be jointed to the old stock and freshly grow; then shall Posthumus end his miseries, Britain be fortunate and flourish in peace and plenty."

'Tis still a dream, or else such stuff as madmen
Toungue and brain not; either both or nothing;
Or senseless speaking or a speaking such
As sense cannot untie. Be it what it is,
The action of my life is like it, which
I'll keep, if but for sympathy.

Play: *Love's Labour's Lost*
Character: Biron
Genre: Comedy
Tone: Comic
Style: Verse
Act/Scene: V ii
Approx. Run Time: .50
Scene Setting: Biron promies Rosaline that he will no longer use trickery to woo her.

———➤●◀———

Thus pour the stars down plagues for perjury.
Can any face of brass hold longer out?
Here stand I: lady, dart thy skill at me;
Bruise me with scorn, confound me with a flout;
Thrust thy sharp wit quite through my ignorance;
Cut me to pieces with thy keen conceit;
And I will wish thee never more to dance,
Nor never more in Russian habit wait.
O, never will I trust to speeches penn'd,
Nor to the motion of a schoolboy's tongue;
Nor never come in vizard to my friend;
Nor woo in rhyme, like a blind harper's song!
Taffeta phrases, silken terms precise,
Three-piled hyperboles, spruce affectation,
Figures pedantical; these summer-flies
Have blown me full of maggot ostentation:
I do forswear them; and I here protest,
By this white glove, — how white the hand, God knows! —
Henceforth my wooing mind shall be express'd
In russet yeas, and honest kersey noes:
And, to begin, wench, — so God help me, la! —
My love to thee is sound, sans crack or flaw.

Play: *Love's Labour's Lost*
Character: Biron
Genre: Comedy
Tone: Seriocomic
Style: Verse
Act/Scene: I i
Approx. Run Time: .35
Scene Setting: Biron protests the King's strict rules of study that he and his friends have agreed to obey for three years.

I can but say their protestation over;
So much, dear liege, I have already sworn,
That is, to live and study here three years.
But there are other strict observances;
As, not to see a woman in that term,
Which I hope well is not enrolled there;
And one day in a week to touch no food,
And but one meal on every day beside,
The which I hope is not enrolled there;
And then, to sleep but three hours in the night,
And not be seen to wink of all the day, —
When I was wont to think no harm all night,
And make a dark night too of half the day, —
Which I hope well is not enrolled there:
O, these are barren tasks, too hard to keep,
Not to see ladies, study, fast, not sleep!

Play: *Love's Labour's Lost*
Character: Biron
Genre: Comedy
Tone: Comic
Style: Verse
Act/Scene: IV iii
Approx. Run Time: .50
Scene Setting: Biron (though secretly in love himself) teases the King and his friends for getting caught in Cupid's trap.

———⇒•○•⇐———

Now step I forth to whip hypocrisy.
   (Advancing.)
Ah, good my liege, I pray thee, pardon me!
Good heart, what grace hast thou, thus to reprove
These worms for loving, that art most in love?
Your eyes do make no coaches; in your tears
There is no certain princess that appears;
You'll not be perjured, 'tis a hateful thing;
Tush, none but minstrels like of sonneting!
But are you not ashamed? nay, are you not,
All three of you, to be thus much o'ershot?
You found his mote; the king your mote did see;
But I a beam do find in each of three.
O, what a scene of foolery have I seen,
Of sighs, of groans, of sorrow and of teen!
O me, with what strict patience have I sat,
To see a king transformed to a gnat!
To see great Hercules whipping a gig,
And profound Solomon to tune a jig,
And Nestor play at push-pin with the boys,
And critic Timon laugh at idle toys!
Where lies thy grief, O, tell me, good Dumain?
And gentle Longaville, where lies thy pain?
And where my liege's? all about the breast:
A caudle, ho!

Play: *Love's Labour's Lost*
Character: Biron
Genre: Comedy
Tone: Comic
Style: Verse
Act/Scene: V ii
Approx. Run Time: .45
Scene Setting: Biron is amazed at Boyet's gift of being able to talk anyone into anything.

This fellow pecks up wit as pigeons pease,
And utters it again when God doth please:
He is wit's pedler, and retails his wares
At wakes and wassails, meetings, markets, fairs;
And we that sell by gross, the Lord doth know,
Have not the grace to grace it with such show.
This gallant pins the wenches on his sleeve;
Had he been Adam, he had tempted Eve;
A' can carve too, and lisp: why, this is he
That kiss'd his hand away in courtesy;
This is the ape of form, monsieur the nice,
That, when he plays at tables, chides the dice
In honourable terms: nay, he can sing
A mean most meanly; and in ushering
Mend him who can: the ladies call him sweet;
The stairs, as he treads on them, kiss his feet:
This is the flower that smiles on every one,
To show his teeth as white as whale's bone;
And consciences, that will not die in debt,
Pay him the due of honey-tongued Boyet.

Play: *Love's Labour's Lost*
Character: Biron
Genre: Comedy
Tone: Comic
Style: Verse
Act/Scene: III i
Approx. Run Time: .30
Scene Setting: Biron rails against falling in love, although it is too late.

What, I! I love! I sue! I seek a wife!
A woman, that is like a German clock,
Still a-repairing, ever out of frame,
And never going aright, being a watch,
But being watch'd that it may still go right!
Nay, to be perjured, which is worst of all;
And, among three, to love the worst of all;
A whitely wanton with a velvet brow,
With two pitch-balls stuck in her face for eyes;
Ay, and by heaven, one that will do the deed
Though Argus were her eunuch and her guard:
And I to sigh for her! to watch for her!
To pray for her! Go to; it is a plague
That Cupid will impose for my neglect
Of his almighty dreadful little might.
Well, I will love, write, sigh, pray, sue and groan:
Some men must love my lady and some Joan.
　　(Exit.)

Play: *Measure for Measure*
Character: Claudio
Genre: Comedy
Tone: Serious
Style: Verse
Act/Scene: III i
Approx. Run Time: .30
Scene Setting: Claudio insists that death is worse than dishonor.

Ay, but to die, and go we know not where;
To lie in cold obstruction and to rot;
This sensible warm motion to become
A kneaded clod; and the delighted spirit
To bathe in fiery floods, or to reside
In thrilling region of thick-ribbed ice;
To be imprison'd in the viewless winds,
And blown with restless violence round about
The pendent world; or to be worse than worst
Of those that lawless and incertain thought
Imagine howling: — 'tis too horrible!
The weariest and most loathed worldly life
That age, ache, penury, and imprisonment
Can lay on nature is a paradise
To what we fear of death.

Play: *Measure for Measure*
Character: Claudio
Genre: Comedy
Tone: Serious
Style: Verse
Act/Scene: I ii
Approx. Run Time: 1.20
Scene Setting: Claudio explains that he has been put in jail for getting his fiancée pregnant; he asks Lucio to persuade Claudio's sister to intercede.

Thus stands it with me: upon a true contract
I got possession of Julietta's bed:
You know the lady; she is fast my wife,
Save that we do the denunciation lack
Of outward order: this we came not to,
Only for propagation of a dower
Remaining in the coffer of her friends;
From whom we thought it meet to hide our love
Till time had made them for us. But it chances
The stealth of our most mutual entertainment
With character too gross is writ on Juliet.
    (* * *)
Unhappily, even so.
And the new deputy now for the duke —
Whether it be the fault and glimpse of newness,
Or whether that the body public be
A horse whereon the governor doth ride,
Who, newly in the seat, that it may know
He can command, lets it straight feel the spur;
Whether the tyranny be in his place,
Or in his emmence that fills it up,
I stagger in: — but this new governor
Awakes me all the enrolled penalties

Which have, like unscour'd armour, hung by the wall
So long that nineteen zodiacs have gone round
And none of them been worn; and, for a name,
Now puts the drowsy and neglected act
Freshly on me: 'tis surely for a name.

   (* *)*

I have done so, but he's not to be found.
I prithee, Lucio, do me this kind service:
This day my sister should the cloister enter
And there receive her approbation:
Acquaint her with the danger of my state:
Implore her, in my voice, that she make friends
To the strict deputy; bid herself assay him:
I have great hope in that; for in her youth
There is a prone and speechless dialect,
Such as move men; beside, she hath prosperous art
When she will play with reason and discourse,
And well she can persuade.

Play: *Much Ado About Nothing*
Character: Benedick
Genre: Comedy
Tone: Comic
Style: Prose
Act/Scene: II i
Approx. Run Time: 1.00
Scene Setting: Benedick was in disguise when Beatrice launched into a speech about how awful he was; now he seethes at what she said.

O, she misused me past the endurance of a block! an oak but with one green leaf on it would have answered her; my very visor began to assume life and scold with her. She told me, not thinking I had been myself, that I was the prince's jester, that I was duller than a great thaw; huddling jest upon jest with such impossible conveyance upon me that I stood like a man at a mark, with a whole army shooting at me. She speaks poniards, and every word stabs: if her breath were as terrible as her terminations, there were no living near her; she would infect to the north star. I would not marry her, though she were endowed with all that Adam had left him before he transgressed: she would have made Hercules have turned spit, yea, and have cleft his club to make the fire too. Come, talk not of her: you shall find her the infernal Ate in good apparel. I would to God some scholar would conjure her; for certainly, while she is here, a man may live as quiet in hell as in a sanctuary; and people sin upon purpose, because they would go thither; so, indeed, all disquiet, horror, and perturbation follows her.

Play: *Much Ado About Nothing*
Character: Benedick
Genre: Comedy
Tone: Comic
Style: Prose
Act/Scene: II iii
Approx. Run Time: 1.05
Scene Setting: Benedick has just overheard his friends gossiping that Beatrice is in love with him even though he's been "mean" to her; he decides it's true and vows to reciprocate.

This can be no trick: the conference was sadly borne. They have the truth of this from Hero. They seem to pity the lady: it seems her affections have their full bent. Love me! why, it must be requited. I hear how I am censured: they say I will bear myself proudly, if I perceive the love come from her; they say too that she will rather die than give any sign of affection. I did never think to marry: I must not seem proud: happy are they that hear their detractions, and can put them to mending. They say the lady is fair, — 'tis a truth, I can bear them witness; and virtuous, — 'tis so, I cannot reprove it; and wise, but for loving me, — by my troth, it is no addition to her wit, nor no great argument of her folly, for I will be horribly in love with her. I may chance have some odd quirks and remnants of wit broken on me, because I have railed so long against marriage: but doth not the appetite alter? a man loves the meat in his youth that he cannot endure in his age. Shall quips and sentences and these paper bullets of the brain awe a man from the career of his humour? No, the world must be peopled. When I said I would die a bachelor, I did not think I should live till I were married. Here comes Beatrice. By this day! she's a fair lady: I do spy some marks of love in her.

Play: *Much Ado About Nothing*
Character: Borachio
Genre: Comedy
Tone: Seriocomic
Style: Prose
Act/Scene: III iii
Approx. Run Time: 1.00
Scene Setting: After going off on a tangent about people being "slaves to fashion," Borachio reports he has successfully played his part in the plan to dishonor Hero, and the result.

Seest thou not, I say, what a deformed thief this fashion is? how giddily a' turns about all the hot bloods between fourteen and five-and-thirty? sometimes fashioning them like Pharaoh's soldiers in the reechy painting, sometime like god Bel's priests in the old church-window, sometime like the shaven Hercules in the smirched worm-eaten tapestry, where his codpiece seems as massy as his club?

(* * *)

Not so, neither: but know that I have to-night wooed Margaret, the Lady Hero's gentlewoman, by the name of Hero: she leans me out at her mistress' chamber-window, bids me a thousand times good night, — I tell this tale vilely: — I should first tell thee how the prince, Claudio and my master, planted and placed and possessed by my master Don John, saw afar off in the orchard this amiable encounter.

(* * *)

Two of them did, the prince and Claudio; but the devil my master knew she was Margaret; and partly by his oaths, which first possessed them, partly by the dark night, which did deceive them, but chiefly by my villany, which did confirm any slander that Don John had made, away went Claudio enraged; swore he would meet her, as he was appointed, next morning at the temple, and there, before the whole congregation, shame her with what he saw o'er night, and send her home again without a husband.

Play: *Much Ado About Nothing*
Character: Borachio
Genre: Comedy
Tone: Serious
Style: Prose
Act/Scene: V i
Approx. Run Time: .30
Scene Setting: Borachio confesses his part in the plan to dishonor Hero, which he believes resulted in her death.

Sweet prince, let me go no farther to mine answer: do you hear me, and let this count kill me. I have deceived even your very eyes: what your wisdoms could not discover, these shallow fools have brought to light: who, in the night, overheard me confessing to this man, how Don John your brother incensed me to slander the Lady Hero; how you were brought into the orchard, and saw me court Margaret in Hero's garments: how you disgraced her, when you should marry her: my villany they have upon record; which I had rather seal with my death than repeat over to my shame. The lady is dead upon mine and my master's false accusation; and, briefly, I desire nothing but the reward of a villain.

Play: *The Comedy of Errors*
Character: Antipholus of Syracuse
Genre: Comedy
Tone: Serious
Style: Verse
Act/Scene: I ii
Approx. Run Time: .20
Scene Setting: Antipholus is lost in Ephesus looking for his family.

He that commends me to mine own content
Commends me to the thing I cannot get.
I to the world am like a drop of water,
That in the ocean seeks another drop;
Who, falling there to find his fellow forth,
Unseen, inquisitive, confounds himself:
So I, to find a mother and a brother,
In quest of them, unhappy, lose myself.

Play: *The Comedy of Errors*
Character: Antipholus of Syracuse
Genre: Comedy
Tone: Seriocomic
Style: Verse
Act/Scene: I ii
Approx. Run Time: .25
Scene Setting: Being unknowingly mistaken for his twin brother takes a toll on Antipholus.

———◆———

Upon my life, by some device or other
The villain is o'er-raught of all my money.
They say this town is full of cozenage;
As, nimble jugglers that deceive the eye,
Dark-working sorcerers that change the mind,
Soul-killing witches that deform the body,
Disguised cheaters, prating mountebanks,
And many such-like liberties of sin:
If it prove so, I will be gone the sooner.
I'll to the Centaur, to go seek this slave:
I greatly fear my money is not safe.

Play: *The Comedy of Errors*
Character: Dromio of Ephesus
Genre: Comedy
Tone: Seriocomic
Style: Prose
Act/Scene: IV iv
Approx. Run Time: .30
Scene Setting: Dromio feels his master treats him no better than livestock.

———⟫•⟪———

I am an ass, indeed; you may prove it by my long ears. I have served him from the hour of my nativity to this instant, and have nothing at his hands for my service but blows. When I am cold, he heats me with beating; when I am warm, he cools me with beating: I am waked with it when I sleep; raised with it when I sit; driven out of doors with it when I go from home; welcomed home with it when I return: nay, I bear it on my shoulders, as a beggar wont her brat; and, I think, when he hath lamed me, I shall beg with it from door to door.

Play: *The Merchant of Venice*
Character: Bassanio
Genre: Comedy
Tone: Serious
Style: Verse
Act/Scene: III ii
Approx. Run Time: .45
Scene Setting: After winning Portia's hand in marriage, Bassanio confesses that all his money was tied up in a venture involving cargo arriving by ship, a ship he has just discovered has wrecked at sea.

—————⇒•⇐—————

O sweet Portia,
Here are a few of the unpleasant'st words
That ever blotted paper! Gentle lady,
When I did first impart my love to you,
I freely told you, all the wealth I had
Ran in my veins, I was a gentleman;
And then I told you true: and yet, dear lady,
Rating myself at nothing, you shall see
How much I was a braggart. When I told you
My state was nothing, I should then have told you
That I was worse than nothing; for, indeed,
I have engaged myself to a dear friend,
Engaged my friend to his mere enemy,
To feed my means. Here is a letter, lady;
The paper as the body of my friend,
And every word in it a gaping wound,
Issuing life-blood. But is it true, Salerio?
Have all his ventures fail'd? What, not one hit?
From Tripolis, from Mexico, and England,
From Lisbon, Barbary, and India?
And not one vessel 'scape the dreadful touch
Of merchant-marring rocks?

Play: *The Merchant of Venice*
Character: Bassanio
Genre: Comedy
Tone: Seriocomic
Style: Verse
Act/Scene: V i
Approx. Run Time: .40
Scene Setting: Bassanio explains how he lost the ring Portia gave him.

———◦———

Sweet Portia,
If you did know to whom I gave the ring,
If you did know for whom I gave the ring
And would conceive for what I gave the ring,
And how unwillingly I left the ring,
When nought would be accepted but the ring,
You would abate the strength of your displeasure.
    (* *)*
No, by my honour, madam, by my soul,
No woman had it, but a civil doctor,
Which did refuse three thousand ducats of me,
And begg'd the ring; the which I did deny him,
And suffer'd him to go displeased away;
Even he that did uphold the very life
Of my dear friend. What should I say, sweet lady?
I was enforced to send it after him;
I was beset with shame and courtesy;
My honour would not let ingratitude
So much besmear it. Pardon me, good lady;
For, by these blessed candles of the night,
Had you been there, I think you would have begg'd
The ring of me to give the worthy doctor.

Play: *The Merchant of Venice*
Character: Bassanio
Genre: Comedy
Tone: Serious
Style: Verse
Act/Scene: I i
Approx. Run Time: .25
Scene Setting: Bassanio asks Antonio for help in finding a way out of debt.

————➤•◆———

'Tis not unknown to you, Antonio,
How much I have disabled mine estate,
By something showing a more swelling port
Than my faint means would grant continuance:
Nor do I now make moan to be abridged
From such a noble rate; but my chief care
Is, to come fairly off from the great debts,
Wherein my time, something too prodigal,
Hath left me gaged. To you, Antonio,
I owe the most, in money and in love;
And from your love I have a warranty
To unburden all my plots and purposes
How to get clear of all the debts I owe.

Play: *The Merchant of Venice*
Character: Bassanio
Genre: Comedy
Tone: Seriocomic
Style: Verse
Act/Scene: III ii
Approx. Run Time: 1.20
Scene Setting: Bassanio chooses the correct casket and wins the hand of Portia in marriage.

———❖———

What find I here?
    (Opening the leaden casket.)
Fair Portia's counterfeit! What demi-god
Hath come so near creation? Move these eyes?
Or whether, riding on the balls of mine,
Seem they in motion? Here are sever'd lips,
Parted with sugar breath: so sweet a bar
Should sunder such sweet friends. Here in her hairs
The painter plays the spider, and hath woven
A golden mesh to entrap the hearts of men,
Faster than gnats in cobwebs: but her eyes, —
How could he see to do them? having made one,
Methinks it should have power to steal both his
And leave itself unfurnish'd. Yet look, how far
The substance of my praise doth wrong this shadow
In underprizing it, so far this shadow
Doth limp behind the substance. Here's the scroll,
The continent and summary of my fortune.
    (Reads.)
"You that choose not by the view,
Chance as fair and choose as true!
Since this fortune falls to you,
Be content and seek no new,
If you be well pleased with this,

And hold your fortune for your bliss,
Turn you where your lady is,
And claim her with a loving kiss."

A gentle scroll. Fair lady, by your leave;
I come by note, to give and to receive.
Like one of two contending in a prize,
That thinks he hath done well in people's eyes,
Hearing applause and universal shout,
Giddy in spirit, still gazing in a doubt
Whether these pearls of praise be his or no;
So, thrice fair lady, stand I, even so;
As doubtful whether what I see be true,
Until confirm'd, sign'd, ratified by you.

Play: *The Merchant of Venice*
Character: Lorenzo
Genre: Comedy
Tone: Serious
Style: Verse
Act/Scene: V i
Approx. Run Time: 1.20
Scene Setting: Lorenzo explains the power of music to Jessica.

How sweet the moonlight sleeps upon this bank!
Here will we sit and let the sounds of music
Creep in our ears: soft stillness and the night
Become the touches of sweet harmony.
Sit, Jessica. Look how the floor of heaven
Is thick inlaid with patines of bright gold:
There's not the smallest orb which thou behold'st
But in his motion like an angel sings,
Still quiring to the young-eyed cherubins;
Such harmony is in immortal souls;
But whilst this muddy vesture of decay
Doth grossly close it in, we cannot hear it.
    (Enter Musicians.)
Come, ho! and wake Diana with a hymn!
With sweetest touches pierce your mistress' ear,
And draw her home with music.
    (Music.)
    (* * *)
The reason is, your spirits are attentive:
For do but note a wild and wanton herd,
Or race of youthful and unhandled colts,
Fetching mad bounds, bellowing and neighing loud,
Which is the hot condition of their blood;
If they but hear perchance a trumpet sound,
Or any air of music touch their ears,

You shall perceive them make a mutual stand,
Their savage eyes turn'd to a modest gaze
By the sweet power of music: therefore the poet
Did feign that Orpheus drew trees, stones and floods;
Since nought so stockish, hard and full of rage,
But music for the time doth change his nature.
The man that hath no music in himself,
Nor is not moved with concord of sweet sounds,
Is fit for treasons, stratagems and spoils;
The motions of his spirit are dull as night
And his affections dark as Erebus:
Let no such man be trusted. Mark the music.

Play: *The Taming of the Shrew*
Character: Biondello
Genre: Comedy
Tone: Comic
Style: Prose
Act/Scene: III ii
Approx. Run Time: .50
Scene Setting: Biondello describes how Petruchio arrives for his wedding looking a mess.

Why, Petruchio is coming in a new hat and an old jerkin, a pair of old breeches thrice turned, a pair of boots that have been candle-cases, one buckled, another laced, an old rusty sword ta'en out of the town-armoury, with a broken hilt, and chapeless; with two broken points: his horse hipped with an old mothy saddle and stirrups of no kindred; besides, possessed with the glanders and like to mose in the chine; troubled with the lampass, infected with the fashions, full of windgalls, sped with spavins, rayed with the yellows, past cure of the fives, stark spoiled with the staggers, begnawn with the bots, swayed in the back and shoulder-shotten; near-legged before and with a half-cheeked bit and a head-stall of sheep's leather which, being restrained to keep him from stumbling, hath been often burst and now repaired with knots; one girth six times pieced and a woman's crupper of velure, which hath two letters for her name fairly set down in studs, and here and there pieced with packthread.

Play: *The Taming of the Shrew*
Character: Petruchio
Genre: Comedy
Tone: Seriocomic
Style: Prose
Act/Scene: IV i
Approx. Run Time: .50
Scene Setting: Petruchio explains how he will break the independence of his wife — "tame the shrew."

⟹•◉•⟸

Thus have I politicly begun my reign
And 'tis my hope to end successfully.
My falcon now is sharp and passing empty;
And till she stoop she must not be full-gorged,
For then she never looks upon her lure.
Another way I have to man my haggard,
To make her come and know her keeper's call,
That is, to watch her, as we watch these kites
That bate and beat and will not be obedient.
She eat no meat to-day, nor none shall eat;
Last night she slept not, nor to-night she shall not;
As with the meat, some undeserved fault
I'll find about the making of the bed;
And here I'll fling the pillow, there the bolster,
This way the coverlet, another way the sheets:
Ay, and amid this hurly I intend
That all is done in reverend care of her;
And in conclusion she shall watch all night:
And if she chance to nod, I'll rail and brawl
And with the clamour keep her still awake.
This is a way to kill a wife with kindness;
And thus I'll curb her mad and headstrong humour.
He that knows better how to tame a shrew,
Now let him speak: 'tis charity to show.
(Exit.)

Play: *The Winter's Tale*
Character: Florizel
Genre: Comedy
Tone: Seriocomic
Style: Prose
Act/Scene: IV iv
Approx. Run Time: .25
Scene Setting: Florizel praises his love, Perdita.

What you do
Still betters what is done. When you speak, sweet,
I'ld have you do it ever: when you sing,
I'ld have you buy and sell so, so give alms,
Pray so; and, for the ordering your affairs,
To sing them too: when you do dance, I wish you
A wave o' the sea, that you might ever do
Nothing but that; move still, still so,
And own no other function: each your doing,
So singular in each particular,
Crowns what you are doing in the present deed,
That all your acts are queens.

Play: *Troilus and Cressida*
Character: Troilus
Genre: Comedy
Tone: Seriocomic
Style: Verse
Act/Scene: I i
Approx. Run Time: .35
Scene Setting: Troilus describes his love for Cressida.

O Pandarus! I tell thee, Pandarus, —
When I do tell thee, there my hopes lie drown'd,
Reply not in how many fathoms deep
They lie indrench'd. I tell thee I am mad
In Cressid's love: thou answer'st 'she is fair';
Pour'st in the open ulcer of my heart
Her eyes, her hair, her cheek, her gait, her voice,
Handlest in thy discourse, O, that her hand,
In whose comparison all whites are ink
Writing their own reproach, to whose soft seizure
The cygnet's down is harsh, and spirit of sense
Hard as the palm of ploughman: this thou tell'st me,
As true thou tell'st me, when I say I love her;
But, saying thus, instead of oil and balm,
Thou lay'st in every gash that love hath given me
The knife that made it.

Play: *Twelfth Night*
Character: Sebastian
Genre: Comedy
Tone: Seriocomic
Style: Prose
Act/Scene: IV iii
Approx. Run Time: .45
Scene Setting: After a wreck at sea, Sebastian has washed ashore (with Antonio, from whom he is separated) at a town where his twin sister has been posing as a boy named Cesario. Since they are identical twins, Sebastian is mistaken for Cesario and treated by everyone as if they know him — including the Lady Olivia who, in love with Cesario and thinking he has finally come to her, takes Sebastian home. Sebastian awakens the next morning and, completely at a loss to explain these events, decides someone must be playing a trick on him.

————⟫•⟪————

This is the air; that is the glorious sun;
This pearl she gave me, I do feel't and see't;
And though 'tis wonder that enwraps me thus,
Yet 'tis not madness. Where's Antonio, then?
I could not find him at the Elephant:
Yet there he was; and there I found this credit,
That he did range the town to seek me out.
His counsel now might do me golden service;
For though my soul disputes well with my sense,
That this may be some error, but no madness,
Yet doth this accident and flood of fortune
So far exceed all instance, all discourse,
That I am ready to distrust mine eyes
And wrangle with my reason that persuades me
To any other trust but that I am mad,
Or else the lady's mad; yet, if 'twere so,

She could not sway her house, command her followers,
Take and give back affairs and their dispatch
With such a smooth, discreet, and stable bearing
As I perceive she does: there's something in't
That is deceivable. But here the lady comes.

Play: *Two Gentlemen of Verona*
Character: Launce
Genre: Comedy
Tone: Comic
Style: Prose
Act/Scene: II iii
Approx. Run Time: 1.20
Scene Setting: Sir Proteus has decided to leave town and is taking Launce, his servant, with him. Launce describes and acts out a tearful family good-bye for the audience and laments that the only one who doesn't care that he is leaving is his dog, Crab.

<hr>

(Enter Launce, leading a dog.)

Nay, 'twill be this hour ere I have done weeping; all the kind of the Launces have this very fault. I have received my proportion, like the prodigious son, and am going with Sir Proteus to the Imperial's court. I think Crab my dog be the sourest-natured dog that lives: my mother weeping, my father wailing, my sister crying, our maid howling, our cat wringing her hands, and all our house in a great perplexity, yet did not this cruel-hearted cur shed one tear: he is a stone, a very pebble stone, and has no more pity in him than a dog: a Jew would have wept to have seen our parting; why, my grandam, having no eyes, look you, wept herself blind at my parting. Nay, I'll show you the manner of it. This shoe is my father: no, this left shoe is my father: no, no, this left shoe is my mother: nay, that cannot be so neither: yes, it is so, it is so, it hath the worser sole. This shoe, with the hole in it, is my mother, and this my father; a vengeance on't! there 'tis: now, sir, this staff is my sister, for, look you, she is as white as a lily and as small as a wand: this hat is Nan, our maid: I am the dog: no, the dog is himself, and I am the dog — Oh! the dog is me, and I am myself; ay, so, so. Now come I to my father; Father, your blessing: now should not the shoe speak a word for weeping:

now should I kiss my father; well, he weeps on. Now come I to my mother: Oh, that she could speak now like a wood woman! Well, I kiss her; why, there 'tis; here's my mother's breath up and down. Now come I to my sister; mark the moan she makes. Now the dog all this while sheds not a tear nor speaks a word; but see how I lay the dust with my tears.

Play: *Two Gentlemen of Verona*
Character: Proteus
Genre: Comedy
Tone: Seriocomic
Style: Verse
Act/Scene: II iv
Approx. Run Time: .50
Scene Setting: Proteus has left home and fallen in love with another woman, leaving behind his love for the girl-next-door, Julia.

———⟫–◦–⟪———

Even as one heat another heat expels,
Or as one nail by strength drives out another,
So the remembrance of my former love
Is by a newer object quite forgotten.
Is it mine, or Valentine's praise,
Her true perfection, or my false transgression,
That makes me reasonless to reason thus?
She is fair; and so is Julia that I love, —
That I did love, for now my love is thaw'd;
Which, like a waxen image 'gainst a fire,
Bears no impression of the thing it was.
Methinks my zeal to Valentine is cold,
And that I love him not as I was wont.
O, but I love his lady too too much,
And that's the reason I love him so little.
How shall I dote on her with more advice,
That thus without advice begin to love her!
'Tis but her picture I have yet beheld,
And that hath dazzled my reason's light;
But when I look on her perfections,
There is no reason but I shall be blind.
If I can check my erring love, I will;
If not, to compass her I'll use my skill.
        (Exit.)

Play: *Henry IV Part I*
Character: Hotspur
Genre: History
Tone: Serious
Style: Verse
Act/Scene: I iii
Approx. Run Time: 1.30
Scene Setting: Hotspur explains why he, exhausted from battle, was rude to the King's messenger and did not give a straight answer to the King's request.

⇒➤-◦-◄⇐

My liege, I did deny no prisoners.
But I remember, when the fight was done,
When I was dry with rage and extreme toil,
Breathless and faint, leaning upon my sword,
Came there a certain lord, neat, and trimly dress'd,
Fresh as a bridegroom; and his chin new reap'd
Show'd like a stubble-land at harvest-home;
He was perfumed like a milliner;
And 'twixt his finger and his thumb he held
A pouncet-box, which ever and anon
He gave his nose and took't away again;
Who therewith angry, when it next came there,
Took it in snuff; and still he smiled and talk'd,
And as the soldiers bore dead bodies by,
He call'd them untaught knaves, unmannerly,
To bring a slovenly unhandsome corse
Betwixt the wind and his nobility.
With many holiday and lady terms
He question'd me; amongst the rest, demanded
My prisoners in your majesty's behalf.
I then, all smarting with my wounds being cold,
To be so pester'd with a popinjay,
Out of my grief and my impatience,

Answer'd neglectingly I know not what,
He should, or he should not; for he made me mad
To see him shine so brisk and smell so sweet,
And talk so like a waiting-gentlewoman
Of guns and drums and wounds, — God save the mark! —
And telling me the sovereign'st thing on earth
Was parmaceti for an inward bruise;
And that it was great pity, so it was,
This villanous salt-petre should be digg'd
Out of the bowels of the harmless earth,
Which many a good tall fellow had destroy'd
So cowardly; and but for these vile guns,
He would himself have been a soldier.
This bald unjointed chat of his, my lord,
I answer'd indirectly, as I said;
And I beseech you, let not his report
Come current for an accusation
Betwixt my love and your high majesty.

Play: *Henry IV Part I*
Character: Hotspur
Genre: History
Tone: Serious
Style: Verse
Act/Scene: I iii
Approx. Run Time: 1.00
Scene Setting: Hotspur rails against the King for being so ungrateful and cruel to the Percy men, who conspired to kill the previous king to set this one on the throne.

━━━►■◄━━━

Nay, then I cannot blame his cousin king,
That wished him on the barren mountains starve.
But shall it be, that you, that set the crown
Upon the head of this forgetful man,
And for his sake wear the detested blot
Of murderous subornation, shall it be,
That you a world of curses undergo,
Being the agents, or base second means,
The cords, the ladder, or the hangman rather?
O, pardon me that I descend so low,
To show the line and the predicament
Wherein you range under this subtle king;
Shall it for shame be spoken in these days,
Or fill up chronicles in time to come,
That men of your nobility and power
Did gage them both in an unjust behalf,
As both of you — God pardon it! — have done,
To put down Richard, that sweet lovely rose,
An plant this thorn, this canker, Bolingbroke?
And shall it in more shame be further spoken,
That you are fool'd, discarded and shook off
By him for whom these shames ye underwent?
No; yet time serves wherein you may redeem

Your banish'd honours and restore yourselves
Into the good thoughts of the world again,
Revenge the jeering and disdain'd contempt
Of this proud king, who studies day and night
To answer all the debt he owes to you
Even with the bloody payment of your deaths.

Play: *Henry V*
Character: Henry
Genre: History
Tone: Serious
Style: Verse
Act/Scene: III i
Approx. Run Time: 1.20
Scene Setting: Henry rouses the spirits of his men to fight one last, mismatched battle in which their exhausted army will surely die.

———◆———

Once more unto the breach, dear friends, once more;
Or close the wall up with our English dead.
In peace there's nothing so becomes a man
As modest stillness and humility:
But when the blast of war blows in our ears,
Then imitate the action of the tiger;
Stiffen the sinews, summon up the blood,
Disguise fair nature with hard-favour'd rage;
Then lend the eye a terrible aspect;
Let pry through the portage of the head
Like the brass cannon; let the brow o'erwhelm it
As fearfully as doth a galled rock
O'erhang and jutty his confounded base,
Swill'd with the wild and wasteful ocean.
Now set the teeth and stretch the nostril wide,
Hold hard the breath and bend up every spirit
To his full height. On, on, you noblest English.
Whose blood is fet from fathers of war-proof!
Fathers that, like so many Alexanders,
Have in these parts from morn till even fought
And sheathed their swords for lack of argument:
Dishonour not your mothers; now attest
That those whom you call'd fathers did beget you.
Be copy now to men of grosser blood,

And teach them how to war. And you, good yeoman,
Whose limbs were made in England, show us here
The mettle of your pasture; let us swear
That you are worth your breeding; which I doubt not;
For there is none of you so mean and base,
That hath not noble lustre in your eyes.
I see you stand like greyhounds in the slips,
Straining upon the start. The game's afoot:
Follow your spirit, and upon this charge
Cry 'God for Harry, England, and Saint George!'
    (Exit.)

Play: *Henry VI Part II*
Character: Young Clifford
Genre: History
Tone: Serious
Style: Verse
Act/Scene: V ii
Approx. Run Time: 1.20
Scene Setting: At the Battle of St. Alban's, Young Clifford discovers that his father has been murdered; he swears revenge on the House of York.

———◆———

Shame and confusion! all is on the rout;
Fear frames disorder, and disorder wounds
Where it should guard. O war, thou son of hell,
Whom angry heavens do make their minister,
Throw in the frozen bosoms of our part
Hot coals of vengeance! Let no soldier fly.
He that is truly dedicate to war
Hath no self-love, nor he that loves himself
Hath not essentially but by circumstance
The name of valour.
    (Seeing his dead father.)
O, let the vile world end,
And the premised flames of the last day
Knit earth and heaven together!
Now let the general trumpet blow his blast,
Particularities and petty sounds
To cease! Wast thou ordain'd, dear father,
To lose thy youth in peace, and to achieve
The silver livery of advised age,
And, in thy reverence and thy chair-days, thus
To die in ruffian battle? Even at this sight
My heart is turn'd to stone: and while 'tis mine,
It shall be stony. York not our old men spares;

No more will I their babes: tears virginal
Shall be to me even as the dew to fire,
And beauty that the tyrant oft reclaims
Shall to my flaming wrath be oil and flax.
Henceforth I will not have to do with pity:
Meet I an infant of the house of York,
Into as many gobbets will I cut it
As wild Medea young Absyrtus did:
In cruelty will I seek out my fame.
Come, thou new ruin of old Clifford's house:
As did Aeneas old Anchises bear,
So bear I thee upon my manly shoulders;
But then Aeneas bare a living load,
Nothing so heavy as these woes of mine.
    (Exit, bearing off his father.)

Play: *Henry VI Part III*
Character: Son
Genre: History
Tone: Serious
Style: Verse
Act/Scene: II v
Approx. Run Time: .40
Scene Setting: An anonymous young soldier discovers that the man he has just killed in battle was his father.

———⟫•◦•⟪———

(Enter a Son who has killed his father, dragging in the body.)
Ill blows the wind that profits nobody.
This man, whom hand to hand I slew in fight,
May be possessed with some store of crowns;
And I, that haply take them from him now,
May yet ere night yield both my life and them
To some man else, as this dead man doth me.
Who's this? O God! it is my father's face,
Whom in this conflict I unwares have kill'd.
O heavy times, begetting such events!
From London by the king was I press'd forth;
My father, being the Earl of Warwick's man,
Came on the part of York, press'd by his master;
And I, who at his hands received my life, him
Have by my hands of life bereaved him.
Pardon me, God, I knew not what I did!
And pardon, father, for I knew not thee!
My tears shall wipe away these bloody marks;
And no more words till they have flow'd their fill.

Play: *Hamlet*
Character: Hamlet
Genre: Tragedy
Tone: Serious
Style: Verse
Act/Scene: II ii
Approx. Run Time: 2.00
Scene Setting: After seeing an actor give a moving imitation of grief for a character called Hecuba, Hamlet derides himself for not being able to grieve, even though his pain at the death of his father is real. He reveals his plan to turn a stage play into a trap for his uncle, the man who murdered his father.

O, what a rogue and peasant slave am I!
Is it not monstrous that this player here,
But in a fiction, in a dream of passion,
Could force his soul so to his own conceit
That from her working all his visage wann'd;
Tears in his eyes, distraction in 's aspect,
A broken voice, and his whole function suiting
With forms to his conceit? and all for nothing!
For Hecuba!
What's Hecuba to him, or he to Hecuba,
That he should weep for her? What would he do,
Had he the motive and the cue for passion
That I have? He would drown the stage with tears
And cleave the general ear with horrid speech,
Make mad the guilty and appal the free,
Confound the ignorant, and amaze indeed
The very faculties of eyes and ears.
Yet I,
A dull and muddy-mettled rascal, peak,
Like John-a-dreams, unpregnant of my cause,
And can say nothing; no, not for a king,
Upon whose property and most dear life
A damn'd defeat was made. Am I a coward?

Who calls me villain? breaks my pate across?
Plucks off my beard, and blows it in my face?
Tweaks me by the nose? gives me the lie i' the throat,
As deep as to the lungs? who does me this?
Ha!
'Swounds, I should take it: for it cannot be
But I am pigeon-liver'd and lack gall
To make oppression bitter, or ere this
I should have fatted all the region kites
With this slave's offal: bloody, bawdy villain!
Remorseless, treacherous, lecherous, kindless villain!
O, vengeance!
Why, what an ass am I! This is most brave,
That I, the son of a dear father murder'd,
Prompted to my revenge by heaven and hell,
Must, like a whore, unpack my heart with words,
And fall a-cursing, like a very drab,
A scullion!
Fie upon't! foh! About, my brain! Hum, I have heard
That guilty creatures sitting at a play
Have by the very cunning of the scene
Been struck so to the soul that presently
They have proclaim'd their malefactions;
For murder, though it have no tongue, will speak
With most miraculous organ. I'll have these players
Play something like the murder of my father
Before mine uncle: I'll observe his looks;
I'll tent him to the quick: if he but blench,
I know my course. The spirit that I have seen
May be the devil; and the devil hath power
To assume a pleasing shape; yea, and perhaps
Out of my weakness and my melancholy,
As he is very potent with such spirits,
Abuses me to damn me. I'll have grounds
More relative than this. The play's the thing
Wherein I'll catch the conscience of the king.
        (Exit.)

Play: *Hamlet*
Character: Hamlet
Genre: Tragedy
Tone: Serious
Style: Verse
Act/Scene: III i
Approx. Run Time: 1.20
Scene Setting: Hamlet ponders his choices: action, inaction, or death.

———➤•◦•◄———

To be, or not to be: that is the question:
Whether 'tis nobler in the mind to suffer
The slings and arrows of outrageous fortune,
Or to take arms against a sea of troubles,
And by opposing end them. To die: to sleep;
No more; and by a sleep to say we end
The heart-ache, and the thousand natural shocks
That flesh is heir to, 'tis a consummation
Devoutly to be wish'd. To die, to sleep;
To sleep: perchance to dream: ay, there's the rub;
For in that sleep of death what dreams may come,
When we have shuffled off this mortal coil,
Must give us pause: there's the respect
That makes calamity of so long life;
For who would bear the whips and scorns of time,
The oppressor's wrong, the proud man's contumely,
The pangs of despised love, the law's delay,
The insolence of office, and the spurns
That patient merit of the unworthy takes,
When he himself might his quietus make
With a bare bodkin? who would fardels bear,
To grunt and sweat under a weary life,
But that the dread of something after death,
The undiscover'd country from whose bourn

No traveller returns, puzzles the will,
And makes us rather bear those ills we have
Than fly to others that we know not of?
Thus conscience does make cowards of us all,
And thus the native hue of resolution
Is sicklied o'er with the pale cast of thought,
And enterprises of great pith and moment
With this regard their currents turn awry,
And lose the name of action. Soft you now!
The fair Ophelia! Nymph, in thy orisons
Be all my sins remember'd.

Play: *Othello*
Character: Cassio
Genre: Tragedy
Tone: Serious
Style: Verse
Act/Scene: III iv
Approx. Run Time: .30
Scene Setting: Cassio, fired from the army by Othello for reasons he does not understand, begs Desdemona to intercede on his behalf.

Madam, my former suit: I do beseech you
That by your virtuous means I may again
Exist, and be a member of his love
Whom I with all the office of my heart
Entirely honour: I would not be delay'd.
If my offence be of such mortal kind,
That nor my service past, nor present sorrows
Nor purposed merit in futurity,
Can ransom me into his love again,
But to know so must be my benefit;
So shall I clothe me in a forced content
And shut myself up in some other course
To fortune's alms.

Play: *Romeo and Juliet*
Character: Benvolio
Genre: Tragedy
Tone: Serious
Style: Verse
Act/Scene: III i
Approx. Run Time: .50
Scene Setting: Benvolio describes to the Prince the swordfight in which Romeo killed Tybalt.

Tybalt, here slain, whom Romeo's hand did slay
Romeo that spoke him fair, bade him bethink;
How nice the quarrel was, and urged withal
Your high displeasure: all this uttered
With gentle breath, calm look, knees humbly bow'd
Could not take truce with the unruly spleen
Of Tybalt deaf to peace, but that he tilts
With piercing steel at bold Mercutio's breast,
Who all as hot, turns deadly point to point,
And, with a martial scorn, with one hand beats
Cold death aside, and with the other sends
It back to Tybalt, whose dexterity,
Retorts it: Romeo he cries aloud,
'Hold, friends! friends, part!' and, swifter than his tongue,
His agile arm beats down their fatal points,
And 'twixt them rushes; underneath whose arm
An envious thrust from Tybalt hit the life
Of stout Mercutio, and then Tybalt fled;
But by and by comes back to Romeo,
Who had but newly entertain'd revenge,
And to 't they go like lightning, for, ere I
Could draw to part them, was stout Tybalt slain;
And, as he fell, did Romeo turn and fly;
This is the truth, or let Benvolio die.

Play: *Romeo and Juliet*
Character: Mercutio
Genre: Tragedy
Tone: Comic
Style: Verse
Act/Scene: I iv
Approx. Run Time: 1.40
Scene Setting: Teasing Romeo for being in love, Mercutio tells the story of Queen Mab, who infects mankind with the disease of love and madness.

———◦—◦—◦———

O, then, I see Queen Mab hath been with you.
She is the fairies' midwife, and she comes
In shape no bigger than an agate-stone
On the fore-finger of an alderman,
Drawn with a team of little atomies
Athwart men's noses as they lie asleep:
Her waggon-spokes made of long spinners' legs,
The cover, of the wings of grasshoppers;
Her traces, of the smallest spider's web;
Her collars, of the moonshine's watery beams,
Her whip, of cricket's bone; the lash of film,
Her waggoner, a small grey-coated gnat,
Not so big as a round little worm
Prick'd from the lazy finger of a maid:
Her chariot is an empty hazel-nut
Made by the joiner squirrel or old grub,
Time out o' mind the fairies' coachmakers.
And in this state she gallops night by night
Through lovers' brains, and then they dream of love;
O'er courtiers' knees, that dream on court'sies straight;
O'er lawyers' fingers, who straight dream on fees;
O'er ladies' lips, who straight on kisses dream,
Which oft the angry Mab with blisters plagues,

Because their breaths with sweetmeats tainted are:
Sometime she gallops o'er a courtier's nose,
And then dreams he of smelling out a suit;
And sometime comes she with a tithe-pig's tail
Tickling a parson's nose as a' lies asleep,
Then dreams he of another benefice:
Sometime she driveth o'er a soldier's neck,
And then dreams he of cutting foreign throats,
Of breaches, ambuscadoes, Spanish blades,
Of healths five-fathom deep; and then anon
Drums in his ear, at which he starts and wakes,
And being thus frighted swears a prayer or two,
And sleeps again. This is that very Mab
That plats the manes of horses in the night,
And bakes the elf-locks in foul sluttish hairs,
Which once untangled, much misfortune bodes:
This is the hag, when maids lie on their backs,
That presses them and learns them first to bear,
Making them women of good carriage.

Play: *Romeo and Juliet*
Character: Romeo
Genre: Tragedy
Tone: Serious
Style: Verse
Act/Scene: I i
Approx. Run Time: .30
Scene Setting: Romeo is lost in the pain of unrequited love.

———≫·O·≪———

Alas, that love, whose view is muffled still,
Should without eyes see pathways to his will!
Where shall we dine? O me! What fray was here?
Yet tell me not, for I have heard it all.
Here's much to do with hate, but more with love:
Why, then, O brawling love! O loving hate!
O any thing, of nothing first create!
O heavy lightness! serious vanity!
Mis-shapen chaos of well-seeming forms!
Feather of lead, bright smoke, cold fire, sick health!
Still-waking sleep, that is not what it is!
This love feel I, that feel no love in this.
Dost thou not laugh?

Play: *Romeo and Juliet*
Character: Romeo
Genre: Tragedy
Tone: Seriocomic
Style: Verse
Act/Scene: II ii
Approx. Run Time: .50
Scene Setting: While hiding in Juliet's garden, Romeo sees her appear on her balcony.

⇒▷◉◁⇐

But soft, what light through yonder window breaks?
It is the east, and Juliet is the sun.
Arise, fair sun, and kill the envious moon,
Who is already sick and pale with grief,
That thou her maid art far more fair than she:
Be not her maid, since she is envious;
Her vestal livery is but sick and green,
And none but fools do wear it; cast it off.
It is my lady; O, it is my love!
O, that she knew she were!
She speaks yet she says nothing: what of that?
Her eye discourses; I will answer it.
I am too bold, 'tis not to me she speaks:
Two of the fairest stars in all the heaven,
Having some business, do intreat her eyes
To twinkle in their spheres till they return.
What if her eyes were there, they in her head?
The brightness of her cheek would shame those stars,
As daylight doth a lamp; her eyes in heaven
Would through the airy region stream so bright
That birds would sing and think it were not night.
See, how she leans her cheek upon her hand!
O, that I were a glove upon that hand,
That I might touch that cheek!

Play: *Romeo and Juliet*
Character: Romeo
Genre: Tragedy
Tone: Serious
Style: Verse
Act/Scene: V iii
Approx. Run Time: 1.50
Scene Setting: Having returned upon hearing the rumor that Juliet is dead, Romeo fights with a man outside the crypt and kills him. He agrees to bury him inside the crypt with Juliet, and he then discovers the man is Paris, who was to marry her. He lays out Paris' body, and then he finds Juliet and swallows poison.

In faith, I will. Let me peruse this face.
Mercutio's kinsman, noble County Paris!
What said my man, when my betossed soul
Did not attend him as we rode? I think
He told me Paris should have married Juliet:
Said he not so? or did I dream it so?
Or am I mad, hearing him talk of Juliet,
To think it was so? O, give me thy hand,
One writ with me in sour misfortune's book!
I'll bury thee in a triumphant grave;
A grave? O no! a lantern, slaughter'd youth,
For here lies Juliet, and her beauty makes
This vault a feasting presence full of light.
Death, lie thou there, by a dead man interr'd.
    (Laying PARIS in the tomb.)
How oft when men are at the point of death
Have they been merry! which their keepers call
A lightning before death: O, how may I
Call this a lightning? O my love! my wife!
Death, that hath suck'd the honey of thy breath,
Hath had no power yet upon thy beauty:

Thou art not conquer'd; beauty's ensign yet
Is crimson in thy lips and in thy cheeks,
And death's pale flag is not advanced there.
Tybalt, liest thou there in thy bloody sheet?
O, what more favour can I do to thee,
Than with that hand that cut thy youth in twain
To sunder his that was thine enemy?
Forgive me, cousin! Ah, dear Juliet,
Why art thou yet so fair? shall I believe
That unsubstantial death is amorous,
And that the lean abhorred monster keeps
Thee here in dark to be his paramour?
For fear of that, I still will stay with thee,
And never from this palace of dim night
Depart again: here, here will I remain
With worms that are thy chamber-maids; O, here
Will I set up my everlasting rest,
And shake the yoke of inauspicious stars
From this world-wearied flesh. Eyes, look your last!
Arms, take your last embrace! and, lips, O you
The doors of breath, seal with a righteous kiss
A dateless bargain to engrossing death!
Come, bitter conduct, come, unsavoury guide!
Thou desperate pilot, now at once run on
The dashing rocks thy sea-sick weary bark!
Here's to my love!
    (Drinks.)
O true apothecary!
Thy drugs are quick. Thus with a kiss I die.
    (Dies.)

Play: *Titus Andronicus*
Character: Demetrius
Genre: Tragedy
Tone: Serious
Style: Verse
Act/Scene: II i
Approx. Run Time: .15
Scene Setting: Demetrius asserts that any woman can be gotten.

———⇒»-0-«⇐———

Why makest thou it so strange?
She is a woman, therefore may be woo'd;
She is a woman, therefore may be won;
She is Lavinia, therefore must be loved.
What, man! more water glideth by the mill
Than wots the miller of; and easy it is
Of a cut loaf to steal a shive, we know;
Though Bassianus be the emperor's brother.
Better than he have worn Vulcan's badge.

FEMALE OR MALE MONOLOGUES

Play: *A Midsummer Night's Dream*
Character: Flute
Genre: Comedy
Tone: Comic
Style: Verse
Act/Scene: V i
Approx. Run Time: .35
Scene Setting: Flute, an amateur actor, performs the female role of Thisbe discovering the slain body of her lover, Pyramus.

———➤•◀———

Asleep, my love?
What, dead, my dove?
O Pyramus, arise!
Speak, speak. Quite dumb?
Dead, dead? A tomb
Must cover thy sweet eyes.
These lily lips,
This cherry nose,
These yellow cowslip cheeks,
Are gone, are gone:
Lovers, make moan:
His eyes were green as leeks.
O Sisters Three,
Come, come to me,
With hands as pale as milk;
Lay them in gore,
Since you have shore
With shears his thread of silk.
Tongue, not a word:
Come, trusty sword;
Come, blade, my breast imbrue:
　　(Stabs herself.)
And, farewell, friends;
Thus Thisbe ends:
Adieu, adieu, adieu.
　　(Dies.)

Play: *A Midsummer Night's Dream*
Character: Puck
Genre: Comedy
Tone: Seriocomic
Style: Verse
Act/Scene: V i
Approx. Run Time: .20
Scene Setting: At the end of the play, Puck steps out of the action to talk to the audience.

If we shadows have offended,
Think but this, and all is mended,
That you have but slumber'd here,
While these visions did appear.
And this weak and idle theme,
No more yielding but a dream,
Gentles, do not reprehend:
If you pardon, we will mend:
And, as I am an honest Puck,
If we have unearned luck
Now to scape the serpent's tongue,
We will make amends ere long;
Else the Puck a liar call:
So, good night unto you all.
Give me your hands, if we be friends,
And Robin shall restore amends.
        (Exit.)

Play: *A Midsummer Night's Dream*
Character: Puck
Genre: Comedy
Tone: Comic
Style: Verse
Act/Scene: III ii
Approx. Run Time: 1.10
Scene Setting: Puck reports to Oberon that the trick they are playing on Titania has been successful. He tells Oberon that he found Bottom near where Titania was sleeping, gave him the head of a donkey, and the love-spell on Titania caused her to fall in love with this transformed man.

My mistress with a monster is in love.
Near to her close and consecrated bower,
While she was in her dull and sleeping hour,
A crew of patches, rude mechanicals,
That work for bread upon Athenian stalls,
Were met together to rehearse a play,
Intended for great Theseus' nuptial-day.
The shallowest thick-skin of that barren sort,
Who Pyramus presented, in their sport
Forsook his scene and enter'd in a brake:
When I did him at this advantage take,
An ass's nole I fixed on his head:
Anon his Thisbe must be answered,
And forth my mimic comes. When they him spy,
As wild geese that the creeping fowler eye,
Or russet-pated choughs, many in sort,
Rising and cawing at the gun's report,
Sever themselves and madly sweep the sky,
So, at his sight, away his fellows fly;
And, at our stamp, here o'er and o'er one falls;
He murder cries, and help from Athens calls.

Their sense thus weak, lost with their fears thus strong,
Made senseless things begin to do them wrong;
For briers and thorns at their apparel snatch;
Some sleeves, some hats, from yielders all things catch.
I led them on in this distracted fear,
And left sweet Pyramus translated there:
When in that moment, so it came to pass,
Titania waked, and straightway loved an ass.

Play: *A Midsummer Night's Dream*
Character: Puck
Genre: Comedy
Tone:
Style: Verse
Act/Scene: II i
Approx. Run Time: .25
Scene Setting: Puck warns the fairies that Oberon is coming, and that he's in a terrible mood because Titania will not give up the changeling child.

The king doth keep his revels here to-night:
Take heed the queen come not within his sight;
For Oberon is passing fell and wrath,
Because that she as her attendant hath
A lovely boy, stolen from an Indian king;
She never had so sweet a changeling:
And jealous Oberon would have the child
Knight of his train, to trace the forests wild;
But she perforce withholds the loved boy,
Crowns him with flowers and makes him all her joy:
And now they never meet in grove or green,
By fountain clear, or spangled starlight sheen,
But they do square, that all their elves for fear
Creep into acorn cups and hide them there.

Play: *A Midsummer Night's Dream*
Character: Puck
Genre: Comedy
Tone: Comic
Style: Verse
Act/Scene: II ii
Approx. Run Time: .25
Scene Setting: Puck has been instructed by Oberon to cast a love spell on the Athenian Demetrius, but seeing Lysander in Athenian clothes, mistakenly casts the spell on him.

⇒•◦•⇐

Through the forest have I gone.
But Athenian found I none,
On whose eyes I might approve
This flower's force in stirring love.
Night and silence. — Who is here?
Weeds of Athens he doth wear:
This is he, my master said,
Despised the Athenian maid;
And here the maiden, sleeping sound,
On the dank and dirty ground.
Pretty soul! she durst not lie
Near this lack-love, this kill-courtesy.
Churl, upon thy eyes I throw
All the power this charm doth owe.
When thou wakest, let love forbid
Sleep his seat on thy eyelid:
So awake when I am gone;
For I must now to Oberon.

Play: *The Tempest*
Character: Ariel
Genre: Comedy
Tone:
Style: Verse
Act/Scene: IV i
Approx. Run Time: .25
Scene Setting: Ariel has brought the drunken conspirators, Stephano and Trinculo, to Prospero for punishment.

———◦———

I told you, sir, they were red-hot with drinking;
So fun of valour that they smote the air
For breathing in their faces; beat the ground
For kissing of their feet; yet always bending
Towards their project. Then I beat my tabour;
At which, like unback'd colts, they prick'd their ears,
Advanced their eyelids, lifted up their noses
As they smelt music: so I charm'd their ears,
That, calf-like, they my lowing follow'd through
Tooth'd briers, sharp furzes, pricking goss, and thorns,
Which entered their frail shins: at last I left them
I' the filthy-mantled pool beyond your cell,
There dancing up to the chins, that the foul lake
O'erstunk their feet.

Play: *Henry V*
Character: Chorus
Genre: History
Tone: Serious
Style: Verse
Act/Scene: Prologue II i
Approx. Run Time: 1.40
Scene Setting: The Chorus, who is our story's narrator, sets the scene for Act II: England is preparing for war with France; all the young men are joining the army; France is nervous and has paid three men to assassinate the King; the scene will move from Southhampton to France.

Now all the youth of England are on fire,
And silken dalliance in the wardrobe lies:
Now thrive the armorers, and honour's thought
Reigns solely in the breast of every man:
They sell the pasture now to buy the horse,
Following the mirror of all Christian kings,
With winged heels, as English Mercuries.
For now sits Expectation in the air,
And hides a sword from hilts unto the point
With crowns imperial, crowns and coronets,
Promised to Harry and his followers.
The French, advised by good intelligence
Of this most dreadful preparation,
Shake in their fear and with pale policy
Seek to divert the English purposes.
O England! model to thy inward greatness,
Like little body with a mighty heart,
What mightst thou do, that honour would thee do,
Were all thy children kind and natural!
But see thy fault! France hath in thee found out
A nest of hollow bosoms, which he fills

With treacherous crowns; and three corrupted men,
One, Richard Earl of Cambridge, and the second,
Henry Lord Scroop of Masham, and the third,
Sir Thomas Grey, knight, of Northumberland,
Have, for the gilt of France, — O guilt indeed!
Confirm'd conspiracy with fearful France;
And by their hands this grace of kings must die,
If hell and treason hold their promises,
Ere he take ship for France, and in Southampton.
Linger your patience on; and we'll digest
The abuse of distance; force a play:
The sum is paid; the traitors are agreed;
The king is set from London; and the scene
Is now transported, gentles, to Southampton;
There is the playhouse now, there must you sit:
And thence to France shall we convey you safe,
And bring you back, charming the narrow seas
To give you gentle pass; for, if we may,
We'll not offend one stomach with our play.
But, till the king come forth, and not till then,
Unto Southampton do we shift our scene.
     (Exit.)

Play: *Henry V*
Character: Chorus
Genre: History
Tone: Serious
Style: Verse
Act/Scene: Prologue I i
Approx. Run Time: 1.10

`Introducing himself as our narrator, the Chorus wishes that a "Muse" would come and transform the play so that it would be as glorious as the true story it tells. But since that cannot be, he asks the audience to use their imagination to turn the stage into a battlefield and actors into kings.

O for a Muse of fire, that would ascend
The brightest heaven of invention,
A kingdom for a stage, princes to act
And monarchs to behold the swelling scene!
Then should the warlike Harry, like himself,
Assume the port of Mars; and at his heels,
Leash'd in like hounds, should famine, sword and fire
Crouch for employment. But pardon, gentles all,
The flat unraised spirits that have dared
On this unworthy scaffold to bring forth
So great an object: can this cockpit hold
The vasty fields of France? or may we cram
Within this wooden O the very casques
That did affright the air at Agincourt?
O, pardon! since a crooked figure may
Attest in little place a million;
And let us, ciphers to this great accompt,
On your imaginary forces work.
Suppose within the girdle of these walls
Are now confined two mighty monarchies,
Whose high upreared and abutting fronts

The perilous narrow ocean parts asunder:
Piece out our imperfections with your thoughts;
Into a thousand parts divide one man,
And make imaginary puissance;
Think, when we talk of horses, that you see them
Printing their proud hoofs i' the receiving earth;
For 'tis your thoughts that now must deck our kings,
Carry them here and there; jumping o'er times,
Turning the accomplishment of many years
Into an hour-glass: for the which supply,
Admit me Chorus to this history;
Who prologue-like your humble patience pray,
Gently to hear, kindly to judge, our play.
　　(Exit.)

ABOUT THE EDITORS

Lisa Bansavage is an actress whose career comprises Broadway, Off Broadway, regional theater, film, television, and national commercial credits, including *Master Class, Law and Order: Criminal Intent, The French Lieutenant's Woman, A Man for All Seasons, The Grapes of Wrath, Grace & Glory, Mastergate, Red Scare on Sunset, The Changeling, The Country Wife, A View from the Bridge, The Beauty Queen of Leenane, The Sisters Rosenweig, Night of the Iguana, A Time to Kill, Married to the Mob, Three Men and a Baby, The Fisher King, Diary of Anne Frank, Vampire Lesbians of Sodom, The Loman Family Picnic,* and a third of the full Shakespearean canon as well as a role opposite Sir Anthony Quayle in the BBC-London production of *An Exchange of Gifts.* She is a graduate of Carnegie-Mellon University's theater conservatory and holds a Master's in Theatre from the University of Pittsburgh where she was a Merrill Fellow. Her Shakespearean stage credits include performances with Great Lakes Shakespeare Festival, New Jersey Shakespeare Festival, Alabama Shakespeare Festival, Three Rivers Shakespeare Festival, Riverside Shakespeare Festival, and the Triple T Theatre Company in a variety of roles: Titania in *A Midsummer Night's Dream* (three times), Kate in *The Taming of the Shrew* (twice), Beatrice in *Much Ado About Nothing* (twice), Desdemona, Emilia, and Bianca in *Othello,* Portia in *The Merchant of Venice,* Celia in *As You Like It,* Lady Capulet, Lady Montague, and The Nurse in *Romeo and Juliet,* Mistress Quickly in *Henry IV Part I,* Elizabeth in *Richard III,* and Viola in *Twelfth Night.*

L. E. McCullough, Ph.D. is an educator, playwright, composer, and ethnomusicologist whose studies in music and folklore have spanned cultures throughout the world. Dr. McCullough is the former administrative director of the Humanities Theatre Group at Indiana University–Purdue University at Indianapolis and current director of the Children's Playwriting Institute in Woodbridge, New Jersey. Winner of the 1995 Emerging Playwright Award for his stage play *Blues for Miss Buttercup*, he is the author of *The Complete Irish Tinwhistle Tutor*, *Favorite Irish Session Tunes*, *St. Patrick Was a Cajun*, *The Complete Irish Tinwhistle Tunebook* and *Whistle Around the World* and has performed on the soundtracks for the PBS specials *The West*, *Lewis and Clark*, and *Not for Ourselves Alone: The Story of Elizabeth Cady Stanton and Susan B. Anthony*. Since 1991 Dr. McCullough has received forty-six awards in thirty-one national literary competitions and has had poems and short stories published 181 times in ninety-two North American literary journals. His books for Smith and Kraus include: *Plays of the Songs of Christmas*; *Stories of the Songs of Christmas*; *Ice Babies in Oz*: *Original Character Monologues*; *Plays of America from American Folklore, vol. 1 and 2*; *Plays of the Wild West, vol. 1 and 2*; *Plays from Fairy Tales*; *Plays from Mythology*; *Plays of People at Work*; *Plays of Exploration and Discovery*; *Anyone Can Produce Plays with Kids*; *Plays of Ancient Israel*; *Plays of Israel Reborn*; *Ultimate Audition Book for Teens, vol. 2*; *Ultimate Audition Book for Pre-Teens*; *"Now I Get It!": 12 Ten-Minute Classroom Drama Skits for Elementary Science, Math, Language and Social Studies, vol. 1 and 2*, *Wild and Wacky Characters for Kids*; and *Software Solutions for the Successful Actor* (with Lisa Bansavage and Dan Jacoby).

Jill K. Swanson is an actor and teacher with the Austin Shakespeare Festival in Austin, Texas. Notable performances include Desdemona in *Othello*, Oberon in *A Midsummer Night's Dream*, Beatrice in *Much Ado About Nothing*, and Helena in *A Midsummer Night's Dream*. Ms. Swanson studied Shakespeare with Jean McDaniel at Florida State University, where her roles included Rosalind in *As You Like It*, Emilia in *Othello*, Hermione in *The Winter's Tale*, and Phebe in *As You Like It*. Nothing has taught her more about performing Shakespeare than teaching kids for Austing Shakespeare Festival, St. Stephen's Episcopal School's Arts on the Lake program.